INSUFFICIENT

PURSUING GRACE-BASED PASTORAL COMPETENCE

RANDY NABORS

ISBN: 978-1-7340181-6-5

Cover design by Sean Benesh

Edited by Julie Serven and Anna Trimiew

FOREWORD

DR. IRWYN INCE

I had no designs on becoming a pastor. Indeed, pastoral ministry was the furthest thought from my mind after graduating from college and starting my professional career. Two and a half years into my marriage, with one young child, I was delighted to begin my career as a systems engineer with a global technology company. I set my sights on climbing the corporate ladder and eventually achieving a corporate vice president position.

A few years into this career plan I was ready to go back to school part-time to pursue a master's degree in business administration. This was a key step to opening the door for management opportunities in my company. Plus, given the company's tuition reimbursement policy, there would be very little out-of-pocket cost for me. As I was researching MBA programs, an idea began to gnaw at me. What about going to seminary instead? Gnaw is the right word to describe the experience because the thought wasn't pleasant. I didn't know where it came from, or why it was now the dominant thought in my mind as I considered furthering my education. The first problem was that this would represent a significant detour from my professional career goals. A seminary degree was not the way to open the door to management opportunities in a global tech company. The second problem was related to the first. My company did not consider the tuition cost of pursuing master's degree from a seminary a reimbursable expense. This change would represent a considerable uptick in out-of-pocket cost! Over those few years into my career, my wife and I now were parents of three children, and she had left her career to be a full-time mom at home.

I recall praying about this decision and literally saying to God, "Lord, I *know* you don't want me to be a pastor! Maybe I'm thinking so seriously about seminary because you want me to become a better Sunday School volunteer teacher." God has a sense of humor. And he is patient with us. It took the better part of a year for me and my wife to be convinced that God was calling me to pastoral ministry. In July 2000 I preached my "trial" sermon at our church in Washington, DC, and began taking seminary courses part-time that fall while continuing to work full-time as a systems engineer.

A year and a half into my seminary studies I found myself in desperate need of mentoring for the pastorate. The Lord, in his kindness, used several people to put Rev. Kevin Smith on my radar. Rev. Kev was planting a Presbyterian Church in America (PCA) church just outside of DC in Bowie, MD. Coming under Rev. Kev's mentoring and pastoral care meant coming into the PCA. One of the blessings from this new denominational connection was the opportunity to also meet and learn from Pastor Randy Nabors. Much of the Spirit given wisdom he has learned through the peaks, valleys, triumphs, and tragedies of pastoral ministry are codified for you in this book. *Insufficient* is a gift!

Pastor Randy is a spiritual father in the ministry for me. I am grateful that his pastoral ministry expanded beyond New City Chattanooga to the wider New City Network in the PCA. This afforded him opportunity to travel and be present over the years in the lives of younger pastors like I was. I saw and see him walk the walk. What you are about to read in the chapters that follow is not an academic treatise, although it should be assigned in the academies that train pastors. It is the wisdom of a practitioner. Pastor Randy writes about the foundational need of the pastor to abide in Christ because he knows firsthand the forces that try to pull pastors away from their first love.

The writer to the Hebrews exhorts his congregation to "strive for peace with everyone, and for the holiness without which no one will see the Lord" (Hebr. 12:14). So, Pastor Randy is right to say that holiness is the one indispensable quality of a pastor. And lest we become confused about what that holiness should look like, he writes:

> I am not speaking here of possessing sanctimonious outward piety or being a self-righteous moralizing poser. I am speaking of a pastor his people will come to know as someone deeply affected by an intimate relationship with Jesus, continually aware of his need and dependence on Christ and full of the joy and confidence that comes from that relationship.

He winsomely leads us through the outflow of this intimacy with Jesus through the pastor's commitment to doctrine, ethics, sound preaching and teaching, shepherding, ecclesiology, cultural awareness and self-awareness. The thought that runs through my mind as I consider what Randy Nabors has offered to pastors and the church is, "For such a time as this." Pastoral wisdom from those who have been tried in the fire is always timely. However, today as pastors must strive for faithful ministry in a culture of contempt, the stakes are higher than ever. We are called to have our feet shod with the gospel of peace, shepherding congregations towards love of God and neighbor at a time of deep cultural polarizations along political lines, along gender lines, in the area of justice, and, yes, even still in the area of race.

I am grateful to God that he provided me a faithful witness like

Pastor Randy, not just to watch from a distance, but to experience his wisdom up close and personal. I pray that through *Insufficient* you receive the same grace. That up close and personal encounter with this faithful pastor. And that the Lord blesses you to glean from his wisdom as you are shaped into a more faithful follower of Jesus Christ.

Dr. Irwyn L. Ince, Jr,
February 2020

Follow whiteblackbirdbooks.pub for titles and releases.

IN PRAISE OF INSUFFICIENT

This is the theology and practice of ministry book I wish I had read in seminary forty-five years ago! Nabors is deeply and uncompromisingly committed to a biblical doctrine that drives him and us to ministry practice in the trenches of life with all of the necessary personal and corporate ethical implications. Wonderful Gospel wisdom pours out of each chapter. It reflects acknowledgement of his own insufficiency yet utter reliance on God's empowering grace.

Mark Dalbey
President and Associate Professor of Applied Theology
Covenant Theological Seminary
Saint Louis, Missouri

In *Insufficient*, Pastor Randy Nabors calls us to the dynamic of biblical faithfulness. He values preaching and concern for the poor, he encourages listening and gentle counsel, and he also calls for courageous confrontation when injustice goes ignored. Let Nabors be one of your mentors, whether you are new to ministry or have spent many years in service. I know I have learned a great deal from him.

Kelly M. Kapic
Professor, Theological Studies, Covenant College
Lookout Mountain, Georgia

Insufficient reveals the heart of a pastor who has learned that we are all insufficient, and without Jesus we can do nothing. I am grateful Pastor Randy is willing to be theological, practical, and autobiographical as he tells his own story and journey as pastor of New City Fellowship.

Wy Plummer
African American Ministries Coordinator, Mission to North America (PCA)
Atlanta, Georgia

From how to preach effectively and handle conflict to how to conduct funerals and weddings, this book covers the pastoral challenges that can leave one feeling insufficient to the calling. From cover to cover, this volume gives good biblical advice.

James Ward
Music Director, New City Fellowship, 2002–2018
Chattanooga, Tennesee

I have known of Randy Nabors for almost twenty years now through the quarterly meetings of our regional church. Randy and his congregation are respected models for pressing the Gospel into areas of justice, mercy, and racial reconciliation. I have found his passion for Jesus, his Gospel, and his church infectious. Let's just say I have admired Randy from afar. I wanted to have him as a teacher, mentor, and friend. And now through his book *Insufficient* I do. It is a must-read for any pastor, new or old, who wants to grow to follow Jesus well and faithfully guide his sheep through hard places into rich pastures. With a keen sense of his own insufficiency and need for Christ, Randy's latest work is clear, timely, challenging, practical, and gracious. If you have hoped for a trusted father in the faith to come alongside you and share out of his own rich life and experience, I commend Pastor Randy and his contribution to the pastoral ministry.

Chris Talley
Pastor, Lakeway Presbyterian Church
Morristown, Tennessee

In *Insufficient*, Pastor Randy challenges us with the truth, and he constantly leads us to the cross of Christ where we find mercy and grace. He has a way of being refreshingly frank about the pastor's daily struggle with the sins of pride, greed, and lust while still encouraging us to apply the Gospel of God's grace in Christ to ourselves. The chapters on cultural competency are especially outstanding. It's an easy read and hard to put down. Whether you're a pastor or a lay person, you will benefit greatly from digging into this nutritious "soul food" Pastor Nabors serves up.

Santo Garofalo
Pastor, New City Fellowship
Atlantic City, New Jersey

Imagine sitting down with a wise, seasoned pastor and talking about ministry "in the trenches." That is the impact of this book. Every pastor, church staff member, or officer will find important insights here. Randy's deep experience in cross-cultural ministry will enhance your cultural intelligence regardless of your context. You don't have to agree with him on everything (he wouldn't expect you to). But you will be equipped to face daily ministry by reading this work.

Bob Burns
Pastor of Spiritual Formation, Church of the Good Shepherd
Co-author of *Resilient Ministry* and *The Politics of Ministry*
Durham, North Carolina

It's been said that legalistic pastors love to lay down the law. That is not what Randy Nabors does in this book, but he does lay down a loving challenge. In this holistic yet brief work, Nabors shares a summary of his decades of experience looking at pastoral competencies through the lens of the cross. Nabors shows us how while pastors are often insufficient for their calling, the sufficiency of Christ can aid us in longterm fruitfulness in ministry.

Daniel Wells
Pastor, Church of the Redeemer
Cortland, New York

Randy Nabors challenges one of the greatest lies within pastoral ministry, the lie that we are up to the task. The greatest gift we can give God's people is our own holiness, desperately depending on God's grace. Do we enjoy our life with God, seen in our prayer life and Scripture reading? If this gives us the impression that the pastor's work revolves around the study, it does not. In fact, that is Nabors' second challenge to pastors. We are to be men of moral courage, preaching the full implications of the Gospel. That involves challenging layers upon layers of sin, requiring personal, emotional, and cultural intelligence. When pastors do this, then we will see churches remembering the poor and working to become the diverse, multicultural family of God that is envisioned in Scripture. I wish I had this book when I was discerning God's call upon my life and am thankful to have it now.

Robbie Schmidtberger
Church Planter, Iron Works Church
West Chester, Pennsylvania

Randy has always been a scrappy stalwart standing in the middle of tension taking hold of two opposing sides and pulling them together. His book *Insufficient* is no different. He brings together the reality of our insufficiency with the demand for pastoral competency, faith with works, doctrine with demonstration, proclaiming truth with providing care, and grace with glory. This book urges pastors to stand in the gap in the strength of Christ.

Kevin Thumpston
Pastor, Watershed Fellowship
Author of *Questions of the Heart*
Lexington, South Carolina

In a day where the calling of the pastor is filled with confusion and uncertainty, Randy Nabors' *Insufficiency* comes across like a bucket of ice water—both refreshing and shocking. This book will challenge those within the conservative evangelical and Presbyterian tradition. It will also reveal theological and cultural blind spots that must be addressed today.

John Bae
Lead Pastor, New Creation Fellowship
New York City, New York

Pastor Nabors is helpfully practical, prophetically convicting, and searchingly insightful. There is a disarming directness to Pastor Nabors that unnerves the self-protective and self-promoting heart. That has been, in my estimation, one of the most wonderful gifts God has given him. That same directness forced me, as a reader to "drop my weapons" and welcome being captured by Biblical truth presented with unvarnished pointedness. I would smile at the courage of many statements and then realize as Nathan said to David, "I was the man" he was describing.
I am 67, and reading books on pastoring has been a part of my life since being ordained about forty years ago. Any book on pastoring worth reading ought to unmask me and assault and even seek to undo anything within me that is not like my Master, Jesus. This book does exactly that, and it does it well!

Joe Novenson
Pastor, Lookout Mountain Presbyterian Church
Lookout Mountain, Georgia

When I was ordained to the Gospel ministry in 1976, Dr. John Sanderson of Covenant College spoke not only to me while giving his charge, but also to my wife, Joan. He compared us to Priscilla and Aquila. While the presbytery was not ordaining Joan, we have always stood together in ministry. For even though the pastor who led us to Christ was concerned that our interracial marriage would hinder our ministry, the opposite has been true. Without each other we surely would not have had the cross-cultural ministry the Lord has blessed us with.

Joan brought into my life a healthy dose of honesty, common sense, and a keen intuition regarding what was good and real. She civilized me, brought much laughter to our home, and through her commitment to our Lord and his church offered a necessary awareness of her people's struggles in this world. Without her there wouldn't be much of me and certainly little impact in the context of our calling. Without her there wouldn't be any music, and I would never get the lyrics right.

So this is for Joan and all that God made possible through her.

ACKNOWLEDGMENTS

A significant foundation was laid through the models and mentors the Lord placed in my life. The pastor that was my shepherd throughout my youth was Rev. Grover C. Willcox, who pastored Calvary Gospel Church of Newark, New Jersey (an independent and interdenominational church). I was blessed with several other ministry influences during that time, including Rev. William (Bill) Iverson, who ministered and pastored in Newark, and Rev. Jim Duffecy and Rev. Art Williams who were evangelists with the Open Air Campaigners. Rev. Don Mostrom and Dr. Richard Lovelace also had an impact during my adolescent years at the Peniel Bible Conference I attended during the summers.

Among the great influences in my life, primarily in ministry focus, have been Evangelist Tom Skinner and Dr. John Perkins of Voice of Calvary and the Christian Community Development Association. Professors and pastors during my college and seminary years, such as Dr. William S. Barker, John Sanderson, Tom Jones, and William McConkey all certainly were influential.

While pastoring in Chattanooga, Tennessee, I had the privilege of belonging to the Black Minister's Union, which later became the Clergy Koinonia. The African American pastors of that group had a great influence on me (I think especially of Dr. Virgil Caldwell and Dr. Paul McDaniel) when it came to ministry, preaching, and church life. I praise God for and am grateful to all of them.

I have also learned much from my peers and younger men. I have worked on staff with several excellent teachers, preachers, and pastors (Dr. Carl Ellis, Rev. Barry Henning, Rev. Jim Pickett, and Dr. Mike Higgins) and alongside pastors in my denomination and in the broader body of Christ (too many to list). I have been sharpened, sometimes rebuked, often inspired, and always encouraged. For all of them (hear me, men from Presbyterian Youth in America, the Tennessee Valley Presbytery, the New City Network, the African American Network, and pastors from Africa, especially in Kenya and Uganda), I give glory to God.

I also am grateful to the man who came after me at New City Fellowship, Rev. Kevin Smith, and the pastor of my home church, Rev. Steven B. Davis. To any of these men who are still living and might be reading this, please know that I am so very grateful for you.

My formal education is a matter of record, and I very much needed the training it gave me. Though some told me I was gifted, and some even said I didn't need to go to seminary, I would have been a poor excuse for a pastor or preacher without it. I give thanks for the late Dr. Robert G. Rayburn, from my alma mater Covenant Theological Seminary, who formally taught me many things about preaching and ministry and was also my friend and advocate. Finally, I offer great thanks to God for the late Mr. Rudolph Schmidt, my first Ruling Elder, without whose sponsorship, advocacy, protection, and coaching I never would have made it past my first years as a pastor.

I am thankful for the hard work and patience of Julie and Doug Serven at White Blackbird Books. Their lives are very busy, and their attention to detail and helpful suggestions and gentle encouragement have been a blessing to me. It is wonderful to have editors who make your work better while trying hard to understand your intentions and knowing that all authors have egos.

CONTENTS

PREFACE

*But we have this treasure in jars of clay to show that this
all-surpassing power is from God and not from us.*
2 Corinthians 4:7

Any discussion of pastoral competence must begin with the reality
of our personal incapacity and the necessity of God's grace. I am a
living testimony of insufficiency, both in giftedness and spirituality.
I can truly say, "Had it not been for the Lord on my side, where
would I be?" (see Ps. 124:1). All pastors are human, and thus
sinners. No pastor has all the spiritual gifts, nor the equitably
balanced temperament, personality, and physical strength to be the
perfect pastor. The good news is that God still calls and uses real,
ordinary, broken people in the ministry!

One of my favorite Bible passages is found in 2 Corinthians 4.
If you are a pastor, I encourage you to remember the things
mentioned by Paul here. Any ministry in which we are engaged we
have only by God's mercy (2 Cor. 4:1). This means that our calling

is a gift, something for which we ought to be grateful. If the Lord gave it to us, we have to believe he will give us all we need to exercise it. We are not adequate in our own resources especially since we did not generate the calling or the gift. In hard times, we need to remember our calling is a gift of mercy.

Part of the struggle of ministry is not only doing it, but doing it with integrity. The Apostle Paul says: *"Rather, we have renounced secret and shameful ways; we do not use deception, nor do we distort the word of God. On the contrary, by setting forth the truth plainly we commend ourselves to everyone's conscience in the sight of God"* (2 Cor. 4:2). God uses weak human vessels like us to show forth his glory and power. As we fulfill God's call to minister to others, we must always remember that this "all-surpassing power" belongs to God and is not from or within ourselves!

One of my church members regularly gave me gifts in the form of sheep that concealed wolves hidden under the sheep's clothing. I know this lady loved and respected me, but it was always sobering to look up on my shelf and see the warning her gifts conveyed. In all seriousness: If you are a pastor but are a wolf in sheep's clothing, stop reading this book and please go resign! Once you have repented and been tested as to your sincerity, then you can pray about coming back into ministry. For I want to make a clear distinction between being an insufficient pastor and being a seducer, deceiver, or crook. The Apostle Paul says in 1 Timothy 5:17–22:

> *The elders who direct the affairs of the church well are worthy of double honor, especially those whose work is preaching and teaching. For Scripture says, "Do not muzzle an ox while it is treading out the grain," and "The worker deserves his wages." Do not entertain an accusation against an elder unless it is brought by two or three witnesses. But those elders who are sinning you are to reprove before everyone, so that the others may take warning. I charge you, in the sight of God and Christ Jesus and the elect angels, to keep these instructions without partiality, and to do*

nothing out of favoritism. Do not be hasty in the laying on of
hands, and do not share in the sins of others. Keep yourself pure.

But for those who are called by God to lead his bride, the
church, take heart that it is God who works in and through you to
accomplish his purposes.

By way of full disclosure, I am a Teaching Elder in the Presbyterian Church in America (PCA). While the PCA believes in
holding its pastors accountable in life and doctrine, it usually leaves
it to individual congregations to hold pastors accountable as to
competency in other areas. In the PCA, Teaching Elders are
known as pastors. In this book, I am addressing those known as
pastors, who have been set apart (paid or employed, bi-vocational or
tent-making) to the full- or part-time job of ministry in the Christian church (1 Tim. 5:17–18).

I am not seeking to defend a particular position on the purpose
of the church, but I also don't think I will be able to hide my incli-
nations as to what the local church should be or should be doing. I
believe in the preaching of the Gospel for the discipleship of people
from all nations. I also believe that all churches should be holistic
both in their understanding of Scripture and in their practice of
Gospel work, including teaching people to observe the commandments and teachings of Jesus in the areas of justice and mercy.

To women who may be reading, in my denomination and theological conviction, the pastoral teaching office is reserved for men. I
may refer to this office as for men, but I recognize that the work of
Gospel ministry is larger and includes more than those in authority
in the PCA. I hope whoever reads this book finds words that are
helpful for the discipleship of the nations, to God's glory.

My inspiration for discussing pastoral competencies in this way
first came after hearing Dr. Carl Ellis speak at a New City
Network Leaders' Summit about the need for a biblical theology
that included both the "A-side" and "B-side" of theology.[1] He
described how the White church especially has emphasized the

3

doctrinal or A-side of theology, while the Black church has historically emphasized the ethical or B-side. From that framework, I
began to think of other competencies that are foundational to
pastoral effectiveness.

While the pastoral competencies included in this book are by
no means an exhaustive list, I hope they will serve as a helpful
guide for those who wish to persevere in long-term vocational
ministry. May this book encourage pastors to fulfill their callings
faithfully while depending on grace and power from God.

---

1. Carl Ellis. Reconciliation & Justice Network Conference, 2016,
"http://www.reconciliationjusticenetwork.com/conferences/2016-confer-
ence/speakers-and-schedule/carl-ellis-2/"

INTRODUCTION

And who is equal to such a task?
2 Corinthians 2:16b

The Apostle Paul when speaking of how God used him to minister the Gospel of Christ asked: *"And who is equal to such a task?"* (2 Cor. 2:16b). The English Standard Version of the Bible translates this verse: *"Who is sufficient for these things?"* Good question, and thus the title for this book, which deals specifically with the insufficient pastor. If you picked up this book because you thought the title described you, congratulations! This might suggest you possess a healthy humility!

Being insufficient as a pastor has little to do with how dumb or smart you are. The truth is that even the most educated pastor can be found wanting in the task of caring for souls. Being smart, intelligent, and educated doesn't mean a person is wise, or fears the Lord, or even has faith. Being smart doesn't mean you have common sense, and you need common sense in spades in order to effectively shepherd souls. In this book, I want to encourage you to pursue grace-based pastoral competence to the glory of God.

To be a great—or even good—pastor you must have a sense of your own inadequacy like the Apostle Paul did. Yet despite acute awareness of personal inadequacy, Paul also had confidence when he said:

> *Such confidence we have through Christ before God. Not that we are competent in ourselves to claim anything for ourselves, but our competence comes from God. He has made us competent as ministers of a new covenant—not of the letter but of the Spirit; for the letter kills, but the Spirit gives life.* 2 Cor. 3:4–6

Powerful ministry is the product of the indwelling of a powerful God in a pastor. God's power is activated in the life and ministry of the pastor through an engaging and dependent faith. It is the Holy Spirit who indwells the believing pastor, and it is only through the Holy Spirit's work that pastors are able to succeed in their holy calling.

My life's calling and vocation has been as a minister of the Gospel, and I have served in ordained ministry for more than forty years, as well as several years in ministry prior to ordination. I have been a youth pastor, church planter, missionary pastor, military chaplain, preacher in prisons, solo pastor of a church, and senior pastor with a staff. I enjoyed the privilege of pastoring one congregation for thirty-six years.

My ministry experience has differed from a typical middle-class suburban pastor. I was brought to Christ in inner-city Newark, New Jersey, and first developed my preaching skills through urban and street ministry with lots of open-air preaching. The church I pastored long-term is urban, cross-cultural, and has intentionally pursued ministry to the poor.

I was ordained in 1976 as an evangelist by the Reformed Presbyterian Church, Evangelical Synod (RPCES). I trained as an evangelist as a teenager and would classify myself as an activist in various kinds of ministry. Today I recruit, train, and coach church planters, and I provide consultation and training for new and established pastors and congregations, especially in the areas of cross-cultural, urban, mercy, and reconciliation ministry.

Though we will discuss competency in the pastoral ministry, I ask that you continually hear the echo of Paul's question in your mind: *"Who is equal [sufficient] to such a task?"* It is a rhetorical question, and the expected answer is: "No one, nobody, and especially not me!"

Then remember that it is God by his grace *"who works in you to will and to act in order to fulfill his good purpose"* (Phil. 2:13).

Pastoral Competencies

But this doesn't mean that there is no craft to your trade that you can and should develop as a pastor. Though vocational ministry is a spiritual calling fueled by the Holy Spirit, that doesn't mean pastors should seek less than other vocations to hone their skills. If anything, pastors should even *more* diligently seek to be competent in the various aspects that will allow them to fulfill the high calling of shepherding souls. God does his work through us, but we need to be faithful stewards in the ministry to which he has called us.

Generally clergy are not governed by bar associations like lawyers or licensed by medical boards like doctors. Instead, Christian leaders possess such a varied level of skill and knowledge that we can't always be sure what we are getting when someone is introduced as a reverend. While churches and denominations may disagree on all the characteristics a pastor should possess, I submit that every pastor should be competent in the following areas for long-term Gospel ministry:

1. Spirituality
2. Doctrine
3. Ethics
4. Preaching and Teaching
5. Shepherding
6. Ecclesiology
7. Cultural Awareness
8. Self-Awareness

In real life, we will at times focus more on some areas than others, but all of them are important. The failure to pursue any of them will lead to deficiencies in our ability to minister. This is not an exhaustive list, but from my years in ministry I do think these are essential. While intellectual capacity, education, knowledge, personality, skills, and gifting vary by pastor, this list can serve as a tool for entities that train, assess, and mentor those in pastoral ministry. It also can help individual pastors grasp a fuller scope of their calling and pursue increased competency in areas of ministry. I admit that I am not perfect in any of these capacities, and I am woefully lacking in some. But by God's grace, I hope to continue to grow in all these areas. You can too!

Assumptions

I want to make clear some working assumptions on my part. First, spiritual ministry must be pursued in the power of God through the work of the Holy Spirit, using spiritual means to accomplish spiritual ends.

Second, men and women are born sinners and need a work of God's grace to come to new life in and through Jesus Christ. There has never been any person ordained to the Gospel ministry who has not been first of all a sinner who struggles with sin. This is true even after he has been washed in the blood of Christ and had imputed to him the righteousness of Christ by faith.

Authentic Christian pastors are saved just as their parishioners are saved—by grace—and they are not pastors by virtue of innate goodness or natural competence. They remain subject to temptation just as every church member is, and they sometimes fall into sin and dishonor their vocation just as some of their church members sin and dishonor their vocations.

However, pastors in biblically faithful churches must be held to a standard of holiness. This moral standard should be even higher than for other believers, since pastors occupy a holy office. We name these: pastor, elder, bishop, preacher, minister, or reverend. That some fail to live up to these standards does not negate the expectation of righteous living that the office carries, even in the opinion of those outside the church.

The Bible sets apart the office of pastor for the good of the church. Some folks don't believe there is such an office and resist the idea of professional clergy. They applaud lay pastors or teachers and don't like hierarchy in their church government. Nevertheless, the office is included among the gifts given for the equipping of the saints and building of the body of Christ in Ephesians 4:11–12 and is laid out throughout the books of First Timothy, Second Timothy, and Titus—appropriately known as the Pastoral Epistles. Whether or not you consider a pastor a professional, he holds a biblical office with God-given responsibilities.

A third assumption is that God calls pastors, but the call has to be discerned and approved by the church, usually by way of a specific call to pastor a particular church. I assume that God equips with gifts everyone he calls, and those gifts are not privately assumed by a presumptuous individual but affirmed by the saints of God. God does call pastors, but the hard reality is that the call must be discerned and approved by a local church.

I have heard a few pastors tell their congregations, "God called me, not you!" as if to say their congregations had no authority over them. This sounds spiritual, but it hints at insecurity. It reveals a power competition between pastor and people, and the writing is on the wall for a firing, church split, or someone leaving. Pastors who plant churches are confirmed in their gifts by the new congregation. Since churches call or hire pastors, I believe they also have the right to fire pastors. Pastors should train their congregations about the process of firing a pastor when and if it ever becomes necessary.

You should gather from this that I don't think an ordination certificate downloaded from the internet qualifies as legitimate. It may make someone legally able to perform weddings, but it has no credibility as to whether he has knowledge, gifts, or character fitting for such holy work. Each calling entity (local congregation, presbytery, denomination, or mission agency) has responsibility to determine qualification by comparing a candidate to the Scriptures (1 Tim. 3:1–7) and their denominational standards.

A fourth assumption: the best way to learn how to pastor is to work under, with, or alongside someone who is good at it. We all need mentors, especially those who will encourage us, give us enough rope to hang ourselves, and then untangle us as they help us analyze how we are doing. *"Walk with the wise and become wise,"* as Proverbs 13:20 teaches us. Good pastoring is caught as well as taught.

This book is not meant to help pastors become more professional while living double lives. Its intent is to encourage authentic Christian preachers to more effectively obey God in their callings, even while admitting their inadequacies. Being a pastor is a holy calling, pursued by imperfect people. Pastors are in the sanctification fight just like all believers. Success in that fight comes by grace through the work of the Holy Spirit in our lives.

To varying degrees, being inadequate applies to all of us. Remember again Paul's question: *"Who is equal to such a task?"* I don't say this to discourage you, because I don't see inadequacy as a disqualification from ministry. Such humility can instead be the foundation of a yearning for grace, which is God's great spiritual power, mercifully given, to do things we cannot do in our own power. My prayer for this book is that the Lord will use it to reveal areas of your ministry in which the Holy Spirit can help you grow. I pray he will use it to bless your life and ministry to others.

PART ONE
SPIRITUALITY
ABIDING IN CHRIST

I am the vine; you are the branches. If you remain in me and I in you, you will bear much fruit; apart from me you can do nothing.
John 15:5

First and foremost, a pastor must know he is deeply loved by God through the saving life and death of Jesus Christ. If a pastor doesn't have faith in Christ, it doesn't matter how competent he is in the other areas. Without faith, his work will at best be ineffective and at worst be damaging to the witness of the church for believers and nonbelievers alike.

Whenever I have been asked by a search committee what they should look for in a pastor, my first response is "holiness." This is one quality that is indispensable. He may or may not be a great preacher, but a pastor will be so much more of a blessing to everyone if he is simply holy, a man who is full of God, who knows, feels, and shows that he is deeply loved by Jesus Christ.

I am not speaking here of possessing a sanctimonious outward piety or being a self-righteous moralizing poser. I am speaking of a pastor his people will come to know as someone deeply affected by an intimate relationship with Jesus, continually aware of his need and dependence on Christ and full of the joy and confidence that comes from that relationship.

Holiness is marked by a man using the "ordinary means of grace," especially time in the Word and in prayer. Yet I have seen men who continually tell others how much they pray, how many times they pray, and how they use the Church Year or the Orders of the Day. Rules, regulations, duty, and discipline are not in themselves the power of holiness. Rather true humility, repentance, a sense of brokenness, faith, hope, and lots of love for others who are broken are the emblematic beauties of holiness.

Unfortunately, there are those who pursue ministry in their own fleshly strength and ambition, and this is not hidden from the people of the world. There are those who use the ministry for their own worldly purpose and who have no real relationship with God or access to his power. Paul revealed almost two thousand years ago something that still rings true today about this kind of abuse of the pastoral office: *"Unlike so many, we do not peddle the word of God for profit. On the contrary, in Christ we speak before God with sincerity, as those sent from God"* (2 Cor. 2:17).

Thankfully, for all those whose faith is in Christ there is great comfort and security. Romans 8:1 says, *"Therefore, there is now no condemnation for those who are in Christ Jesus."* This can be especially comforting news for those of us who are pastors and know quite well that we are insufficient for the work before us. This allows us to minister to others out of an overflow of the security we ourselves experience in Christ and to have an anchor in the midst of the stresses of ministry.

Both in times of stress and times of success we would do well to remember what Jesus tells us in John 15:5: *"I am the vine; you are the branches. If you remain in me and I in you, you will bear much fruit; apart from me you can do nothing."* Is that not clear enough for us to understand our insufficiency? Without Christ in us, we can do nothing!

Paul's corresponding claim that *"I can do all things through him who gives me strength"* (Phil. 4:13) is not arrogance but utter dependence. We too must maintain this confident dependence in our own ministries.

Sadly, some pastors are morally corrupt and some don't even believe in God. Some congregations don't seem to care whether their pastor has any real personal faith so long as he keeps the organization running smoothly, holds to traditions, and doesn't do anything terrible, like sexually abusing children or stealing money from the church. (As an aside, let me say that the horrible exposure of sexual abuse by clergy and the concealing or dismissing of such sins by church leaders means that some have excused even this level of moral corruptness. This is horrific, wrong, shameful, inexcusable, and illegal. Church leaders must never assume that such acts can be treated solely with religious counseling and forgiveness by the victim. Forgiveness is necessary, but probably should be given through the bars of a cell.)

Success in ministry is not always a place of joy and contentment either. Hubris has sent many a pastor into an adulterous affair or to being power hungry and abusive. When people start applauding and complimenting you, lifting you up above other preachers, telling you that you have made *the* difference in their lives, giving you special gifts (cars, club memberships, money for whatever special ministries you want to pursue, vacation trips, etc.), and generally making you feel you are especially anointed by God —then you must watch out for the edge of the cliff there too!

I love this verse from Hebrews 10:14: *"For by one sacrifice he has made perfect forever those who are being made holy."* This is the Gospel's perfect summation of what it means to be considered forever holy by God, in and through Christ, while still being in that furnace of purification known as "real life." May the Lord help us all!

PRAYER

One cannot be spiritually engaged, live, or fight without being in prayer. There are many books on prayer, movements about prayer, and teachings on following certain prayer regimens to give order to your day.

When the Lord Jesus was asked by his disciples to teach them to pray, he gave them and us what is called the Lord's Prayer, or the Our Father. I learned this prayer in public school when I was young. Sadly, now it is rarely heard in some congregations, and our culture is the poorer for losing this common cultural touchstone. It is a text used by many pastors to teach their congregations how to pray, but it is also always a meaningful prayer on its own—at least it is for me.

The New Testament gives us the record and pattern of how the Apostles prayed, and what they asked God to do in them and us, but we are not given formulas for prayer except to do it without ceasing. Simple, right? So that is my word to you; pray, pray all the time, and pray about everything. Pray alone, pray with others, and don't constantly tell others how much you are praying. Stop talking and just do it! When you don't want to do it, pray about that. A living conversation with the Father is what a life of dependence is all about.

There are certain subjects that tend to make me feel guilty. Those subjects are prayer, love, and evangelism. Usually the conviction comes with the word "enough"—as in I know I haven't prayed enough, or loved enough, or witnessed enough.

Developing habits of prayer can be helpful, and each pastor must be mindful of how much he is depending on the Lord for... everything! Yes, every little and big thing in his life. Some make prayer lists, some have certain times of day for certain kinds of prayer. Some pastors are known by their church members as someone who will refuse to have a conversation with them without praying with and for them, even on the phone.

I react to any prayer that is used to send a message, not to God but to others who are listening. As I listen to others pray, I may be encouraged or convicted, but the sincerity of a prayer and its honesty mean so much to me.

I think about how much better my life would have been if I had prayed instead of worrying about things, if I had prayed instead of wondering where the resources would come from, if I had prayed instead of being angry and resentful, if I had prayed instead of muttering about politicians and government, if I had prayed instead of planning how I would solve a problem in the church, my family, etc. How much better my congregation would have been if they (and I) had believed that God answers prayer about our finances, our building, our safety, our missionaries, our staff, the quality of the preaching, and our denomination.

SPIRITUAL WARFARE

Those in vocational ministry should not be surprised when they experience spiritual attack. Satan delights in derailing those who want to bring God glory.

So, what are your sins? How is the devil tempting you? I encourage you to take his attacks personally and get to know his tricks and devices. In order to know his tricks, you need to know where he seems able to get at you. Is it blinding ambition? Is it a lust to achieve status and notoriety as a successful pastor, conference speaker, or author? Is it vanity pushing for more academic degrees, thirsting to be called "doctor"? Do you have an idol of esteem in wanting public assignments to prestigious committees or agencies? Is it envy and jealousy of other pastors and leaders who seem to get invited to speak and preach when you don't? Is it bitterness every time you hear of someone else's success?

Is your sin in the area of coveting material things? Have you given yourself to a love of money and the things it can buy? Is your treasure here on earth? Or is your lust more physical, the lust of the flesh and the lust of the eyes? Is sex your assurance that you are worth something, that you are not alone, that you are loved? Has it become an addiction? Are you fantasizing, using pornography, cheating on your wife with another man or woman?

Do you crave the flattery of men? Do you cave in to the powerful and well connected and live in fear that they will take that adulation away? Or do you love power, the little that you have as pastor over your staff and church members? Do you manipulate people, use anger to control them, and fail to encourage or build them up? Do your fears keep you from listening to people when they give feedback critical of your performance? Are you an angry husband? Are you an exasperating father? Is your sin a simmering anger with God? Have you fallen into the belief (i.e., unbelief) that he doesn't really love you or care? Are you growing cold in your ability to believe?

If you answered yes to any of these, you are not alone. I have struggled with most of them. I sometimes feel I am lazy and not earning my pay, so I become a driven perfectionist and a workaholic. I was actually surprised when my wife pointed out that I have an obsession with work. My sins are nasty and real, and not simply that "I haven't had enough quiet time with Jesus this morning." I have not prayed enough. I have not shared Jesus when I had the opportunity. I have hated others in my heart. And more.

But despite my failure, I know that Jesus loves me. I can't imagine how or why, except that the Bible keeps telling me he does. "Surely," you might say, "how could this man continue to be a pastor?" For the same reason you do, and should. Only real flesh-and-blood people are called to be pastors. They're not angels. Real pastors are sinners who need to repent daily, and yet seek by the grace of God to live holy and in the power of the Holy Spirit. We are indeed insufficient.

God wants you to *"stand your ground, and after you have done everything, to stand"* (Eph. 6:13). Ephesians 6 is a chapter about using and wielding the armor of God, which you will need to withstand the devil. His fiery darts are and will be thrown at you. Wake up and realize you have an enemy who *"prowls around like a roaring lion looking for someone to devour"* (1 Pet. 5:8). You have an outside enemy who knows how to get inside: There, you will struggle with *"the lust of the flesh, the lust of the eyes, and the pride of life"* (1 John 2:16).

One of the devil's tricks is to get you to deny his existence or minimize his power. Another trick is to diminish the power of temptation or make you think you are not prone to it. Satan doesn't want you to pray that you would not enter into temptation, as Jesus instructed his disciples to do. The devil would like you to think your enemy is the person in front of you (your spouse, elder, church member, etc) when it is actually him.

After I became a Christian, I realized that temptation in my life was real, and as I entered puberty and adolescence, I was hardly able to say no to my sinful desires. I was taught about "crucifying my flesh" by some of my spiritual leaders. Unfortunately I fell into a false understanding of how to pursue "victory" in my spiritual life. Sanctification became a series of attempts to use biblical phrases in my prayer life combined with willpower as a means of reckoning myself to be dead to sin.

The big problem was my willpower wasn't willing to die to my sin. It took years for me to understand that my will was as fallen as anything else about me. Holiness doesn't come from strong-willed people, but by people aware that without grace they are helpless against their sinful natures. I didn't need more determination; I needed God's delivering intervention. This is why any kind of discipline is not and cannot be a replacement for the work of the Holy Spirit in a believer's life based on his or her union with Christ.

Real sanctification leads to an existential reality of being willing to die to self, by the power of God, through the work of Jesus in his saving mercy. Holiness is grace-based and activated by faith. Truly believing in the Gospel always leads to holiness. Holiness makes God beautiful, and it is what makes us beautiful as human beings as well.

Holiness is not any kind of religion that substitutes rules, disciplines, or habits for love, joy, peace, patience, kindness, goodness, faithfulness, gentleness, and self-control. These are indeed the fruit of the Holy Spirit (Gal. 5:22–23) and not the fruit of willpower. Holiness is never associated with self-righteousness nor a spirit of being judgmental and censorious. Fundamentalist moralizing is not the beauty of holiness.

Another of Satan's tricks is to make you believe that when you fall you are helpless against him or your addictions. He wants you to believe that your temptation is unique and that God can't and won't provide a way out for you (the opposite of 1 Cor. 10:13). One of the devil's great techniques is to cause you to despair, to believe God can no longer forgive you, that his mercy has come to an end. But Jesus was made known to put to death the works of the devil (1 John 3:8)! Jesus crushed the serpent at the cost of his life, and now the Spirit of Jesus who resides in you is greater—much greater. Don't be afraid. Fight and stand!

As we transition in the next chapters to focusing on doctrine, let me connect it to this section on spiritual warfare. One of the parts of spiritual armor is the belt of truth. Jesus is the truth incarnate, and he taught us that the truth will set us free. Being confused about that truth or deceived about it can create vulnerabilities in our spiritual armor. I believe this has happened to the church when our cultural bias has become not a lens for focus but a blindfold. Our spiritual armor belts must be truth not something masquerading as truth.

SUGGESTIONS

1. Pray. How do you pray? What is your habit or pattern of prayer? What steps can you take to increase or build habits of prayer in your life?

2. Read your Bible. What is your pattern of using the Bible? Do you read it daily for devotion and encouragement? Is it just a text for sermons? Do you meditate on it, think about it? Are you convicted by it?

3. Listen to sermons by others (live, online, and podcasts). Visit other churches occasionally.

4. Listen to worship music that encourages you spiritually. Stay qualified to represent God and maintain your character so that you're worthy to stand at the "holy desk." Keep short accounts with God by being quick to repent when you have sinned and asking God to forgive you. It is better to give over your pastors responsibility to someone else, even for a day or moment, than to hurt your

conscience by pretending to be something you are not. It is wrong to forsake repentance.

PART TWO
DOCTRINE

KNOWING A-SIDE THEOLOGY

*Watch your life and doctrine closely. Persevere in them, because if
you do, you will save both yourself and your hearers.*
1 Timothy 4:16

Some of us may find it hard to admit and confess to being insufficient in our understanding of theology. After all, we may have
spent a great deal of time studying the Bible, reading Bible
commentaries, and attending Bible school or seminary. But before
you decide to skip this chapter entirely, I ask you to consider the
argument of Dr. Carl Ellis that there is an A-side theology and B-
side theology, both of which are needed for a robust biblical theology.[1] We will discuss the propositional A-side in this chapter and
the ethical B-side in the next.

In the Western tradition we usually begin by understanding
theology as doctrine. Getting our theology and doctrine right
(according to our tradition) is essential because we think everything
is built upon it and flows from it. If you have poor theology, then it
is fairly certain the house that is built on this poor foundation will
lean, sag, and perhaps even fall. However, it is both revealing and

convicting to remember that Jesus told us, *"Therefore everyone who hears these words of mine and* puts them into practice *is like a wise man who built his house on the rock"* (Matt. 7:24, emphasis mine). So we see that Jesus teaches it is not solely believing and confessing the right thing that is necessary. Rather there are two indispensable things (like the two sides of a record) to consider: 1) What has Jesus told us to believe, think, and do? and 2) Are we in fact doing those things?

Those who are convinced they have the correct theological positions assure us they know what is right and true. They know with precision what God is like, what he has done for us, and how we should live. Unfortunately, their orthodox theological commitment is neither a guarantee that they themselves are living in all of that truth, nor that they have paid similar attention to the application-to-life parts of their theology. This is why we will speak in the next chapter about the ethical, or B-side, of theology.

---

1. Carl Ellis. Reconciliation & Justice Network Conference, 2016, "http://www.reconciliationjusticenetwork.com/conferences/2016-conference/speakers-and-schedule/carl-ellis-2/"

BELIEVE THE BIBLE

The reality is that even the decision to believe and preach from the Bible as the Word of God is itself a theological choice. Since I have already said that I think a pastor must be spiritually competent and possess an abiding faith in Christ, I am assuming that he also would believe that the Bible is alive and active and a necessary tool in ministry. Hebrews 4:12 says: *"The word of God is alive and active. Sharper than any double-edged sword, it penetrates even to dividing soul and spirit, joints and marrow; it judges the thoughts and attitudes of the heart."*

Paul, under the inspiration of the Holy Spirit, was a rigorous theologian. His thinking and writing were precise, and he considered all of Scripture and saw how things fit together. There are certainly disagreements and arguments about what things mean and how they should be applied, but it is possible to come to a systematic and unifying understanding of the teaching of Scripture.

There are of course topics highlighted in Scripture that are beyond ordinary human experience—such as God becoming man and Jesus becoming sin, dying in our place, rising from the dead, ascending into heaven, and returning to earth someday. Christianity takes faith to believe what is true.

For those who, like me, take the Bible literally, this doesn't mean these events didn't happen. It makes it somewhat straightforward (intellectually speaking) to conclude what the Bible says is true and accurate. The Western tradition in institutional or denominational churches is not so much filled with mysticism as with disagreement over definitions and interpretations. This has led to all sorts of divisions in Christendom and the creation of various denominations and traditions. As Evangelicals we admit this in our hymnody when we sing "The Church's One Foundation" that "by schisms rent asunder, by heresies distressed." Yet there is still a core of agreed-upon truth wonderfully summed up in the Apostles' Creed (see the appendix).

Since the Reformation, Protestant churches have disagreed (beyond their disagreement with the Roman Catholic Church) about the meaning and mode of the sacraments, types of church government, the coordination or interplay between God's sovereign will and humanity's free will, and how to understand the organization of God's revelation of the history of his means of salvation (covenants versus dispensations). But the largest disagreement, and most crucial, is over the authority of Scripture itself.

Once you leave the commitment to an infallible revelation from God in the book we call the Bible, almost any idea or belief becomes possible. This can lead you right out the door of orthodoxy or faith itself. In short, unbelief (or choosing not to believe) in a miraculous history or a divine, authoritative revelation means you have left the religion of Christianity and gone elsewhere, even if still wrapped in ecclesiastical robes. You may yet be a Christian, but it would be hard to justify it intellectually, since you have accepted a liberal and modernistic presupposition that miracles don't happen.

Biblical Christianity is a profoundly supernatural religion. It is based on the idea that God does indeed create out of nothing and intervenes in the laws of physics because he is the one who makes them work in their usual way on a daily basis, until he chooses not to. Science says dead people don't and can't come back. Christians agree that is generally true, but the Bible says Jesus did, and Christians believe his resurrection is not simply a myth or a morality play, but a historical fact. Once you believe in God, why would you think it strange that he could raise the dead (Acts 26:8)?

I am one who believes the Bible, all of it, to be the Word of Almighty God. As with many of my Western peers, I studied the Bible academically, but it has always been more than only an academic book. I still read the Bible devotionally, seeking to hear God's voice, understand his will, and believe his promises. The Bible gives me faith and encourages me, although sometimes it scares me too. I think the fear of God is a clean, good thing for those who love him.

Even if you don't believe the Bible, it is generally clear enough for all to understand. We can agree on the meaning of lots of things if we know the meaning of the words, the context of the arguments, and have some grasp of its historical and cultural context. In short, the Bible cannot be manipulated in support of whatever the reader wants it to say, although religious and mystical people attempt such things. We can listen to preachers and discern whether or not they are being faithful to the meaning of a passage; they are either properly interpreting the text or they are distorting it. I am not trying to be self-righteous and judgmental of others; rather I'm calling for intellectual integrity and honesty. I might believe the passage, and another might not, but it is possible, with intellectual honesty, to at least agree on what the text says.

KNOW THE BIBLE

At the risk of stating the obvious, I am going to state the obvious: If you are going to preach and teach from the Bible, then you ought to know it! The Apostle Paul tells Timothy (and us): *"Do your best to present yourself to God as one approved, a worker who does not need to be ashamed and who correctly handles the word of truth"* (2 Tim. 2:15).

That seems pretty clear. If you are a pastor, you need to know your stuff! To correctly handle the word of truth, you need to know what the Bible is actually saying. This calls for study on the part of every person tasked with preaching and teaching the Word of God.

We can all go to school (formal or not) and learn the books of the Bible and the order in which they have been set. We can learn the flow of each distinct book of the Bible, why it was written, to whom it was written, and what it says. We can even memorize it. Paul tells the young pastor Timothy:

> *But as for you, continue in what you have learned and have become convinced of, because you know those from whom you learned it, and how from infancy you have known the Holy*

Scriptures, which are able to make you wise for salvation through faith in Christ Jesus. All Scripture is God-breathed and is useful for teaching, rebuking, correcting and training in righteousness, so that the servant of God may be thoroughly equipped for every good work. 2 Tim. 3:14–17

If we work at it long enough, we can see how the different parts of the Bible fit together, e.g., how the predictions and prophecies found in earlier books come to pass in later books. We can see a plan from God unfolding as the story is revealed book by book. We can see how some later parts affect our understanding of earlier parts, or how some things have transformed. People ignorant of the biblical story may not see how this progressive revelation took place and tend to view portions of Scripture out of context. They might assume that those who believe the Bible interact with it the same way.

Yes, there is room enough for people to take the same understood meaning and teaching and apply it in radically different ways, and this creates areas for debate and more rigorous study. This is one reason we have theologians, Bible colleges, and theological seminaries. Some denominations (such as the Presbyterian Church in America, of which I am a part) hold strongly to an educated clergy. For them it is not enough for someone to be a caring soul or leader in order to be a pastor. Leaders who are strong, have charisma, seem sincere, and seem to care for their followers yet have little knowledge or understanding of the Scriptures have a powerful platform and can easily lead people into error and trouble. In this way cults have been created, and people's lives and families have been destroyed. We've got to know our Bibles!

INTERPRET THE BIBLE

Since denominations and theological traditions want their adherents to understand and follow their particular beliefs, they understandably train their clergy in the doctrines that define them. This leads to an amazing amount of intellectual and cognitive discipline. Since the Bible is a big book, and since there is so much history in how people have either understood or misunderstood it, there is a lot to study.

Questions arise such as: Who first had the idea that this is what this particular passage means? Who wrote about it? What did that idea initiate in others? Who opposed it? What exactly is the right way to understand it?

A great deal of theological understanding comes by way of oppositional thought. As we analyze alternative ideas, we wonder what the philosophical context of some of that opposition might be. How have some groups translated and interpreted this passage, and what kinds of rituals and behaviors have come out of that? Were they right or were they wrong?

At one point during my ministry as an Army chaplain I had to introduce myself to the Post Chaplain. I saw a few other chaplains down the hall of the post chapel and walked toward them. The ranking chaplain met me and asked what my denomination was, which was not evident on my uniform. This is a fairly typical first question between chaplains, and I had no problem telling him that I was a Reformed Presbyterian. He suddenly became a little frosty in his attitude and said, "Oh, you're those people who always think you are right."

Since he outranked me, I refrained from giving a sarcastic reply, but I've thought of some since then. One reply might be, "Why would anyone want to be in a denomination where they thought they were wrong?" I imagine he was referring more to a self-righteous or superior attitude from some of my brethren than to an actual commitment of conscience to what we believe. I am sorry that this indeed might be so, but it is worse to assume that there is no theological conviction which is true, correct, and biblical. That kind of equivocation doesn't help anyone.

Is everyone equally right (how can that be?), or are there definitely those who are right and those who are wrong? Some really brilliant people think everyone—at the same time—can be right about entirely opposite ideas when it comes to religion, but oppose the contradiction in every other discipline. There is no other discipline in which the stakes are so high, in fact they're eternal.

Whose opinion can we trust, and who do we need to watch out for or be skeptical of when reading their words or listening to them? What are their theological presuppositions? Having been a student at a theologically conservative seminary, I can testify that we did not simply accept dogma or maxims, but in our study considered opposing—and even unbelieving—points of view.

Those who are impressed with learning tend to give status and credibility to those who have spent years in formal school, who have written articles and books, and have academic degrees behind their names. The Western (Reformed) theological tradition is an intellectual tradition, and it has created churches and congregants who stress reasoned discourse, sermons that are like lectures, and speakers who are erudite and quote extensively. There is a corresponding tendency to dislike emotion or emotional outburst from listeners.

In some ways this is a materialistic tradition as it thrives on books, academic institutions, and academic position—all of which cost lots of money. It tends to produce pastors who spend a great deal of time in their studies amid books, who write their manuscripts, and who travel to hear scholars give opinions about subjects they have already mastered.

So is this good or bad? As I have already said, good theology is necessary to create a firm foundation for our understanding and thus our beliefs. But unfortunately, a good doctrinal foundation doesn't guarantee a good life will follow. The Pharisees from the time of Christ are a good—or terrible—example of that way of thinking.

Nonetheless, we absolutely must learn from God if we are to know God and what he desires from us. We must learn these things accurately so we do not believe lies or teach lies. We must be able to discern truth from error so *"... we will no longer be infants, tossed back and forth by the waves, and blown here and there by every wind of teaching and by the cunning and craftiness of people in their deceitful scheming"* (Eph. 4:14). In the world of biblical scholarship, some teachers are in fact wrong in their understanding, and some teachers are deceitful. So there is no excuse. Every pastor has to be a student and has to learn the Bible. They must become masters of their subject as far as they are able.

DANGERS OF KNOWING WITHOUT DOING

But to know theology is not the same as living it! As the Gospel song says, "Everybody talking 'bout heaven ain't going there." The Bible contains warnings. In 1 Corinthians 8:1, we read: *"But knowledge puffs up while love builds up."*

There is so much right about having a passion to learn, study, and grow in theological understanding. Yet an attendant danger accompanies an academic culture. The knowledge of our theology, intellectual defense of our theology, and condemnation of those holding to "bad" theology has sometimes given us a sense of superiority to which we have no right, especially in our (sometimes willful) failure to live out our theology in obedience in all areas of life.

I am not defending anti-intellectualism. I believe all believers are called to study and learn the Scriptures. And whether we have a teacher or read or listen to the Bible on our own, the Holy Spirit makes clear God's truth to believers (1 John 2:20–21). God has made his word approachable. The illiterate can understand the Bible as they hear it recited or told by others. Jesus taught through stories, and the concepts of his life-changing teaching certainly affected the history of the world and the lives of millions. Many believers throughout history have learned in and from an oral tradition and still have held consistently to orthodox belief.

The academic and doctrinal side of theology is a necessary (and often delightful) part of learning the Word of God, though it can come with attendant temptations. You can develop a dryness of soul that comes from replacing a relationship with God (knowing God) with merely learning about God, or being puffed up with a sense of superiority over those who seem to know less than you do. To learn, you must come to know, and knowing what God has said was certainly the passion of the psalmist, but all of it was simply a means of knowing the Lord God himself.

Psalm 119 describes a sort of love affair with pursuing, learning, and knowing the Law of God. Every couplet in the Psalm includes something about the Scriptures. The faithful pastor must also love the truth of God expressed in and through the written Word of God. David writes, *"Oh, how I love your law! I meditate on it all day long"* (Ps. 119:97), *"Your word is a lamp for my feet, a light on my path"* (Ps. 119:105), *"The law from your mouth is more precious to me than thousands of pieces of silver and gold"* (Ps. 119:72), and *"How sweet are your words to my taste, sweeter than honey to my mouth!"* (Ps. 119:103).

To know the Scriptures as a means of drawing closer to God himself is an essential part of being a pastor. It is not knowledge in and of itself, but knowledge in order to have a closer relationship with God through Christ. It is essential to have a strong theological foundation to build our ministry upon. We must know the Scriptures—what they mean, what is in them and what is not, how they are to be applied, how to discern truth from error, and how those Scriptures enable us to be wise unto salvation.

CULTURAL TENDENCIES

Before we leave a discussion of orthodoxy and move to a discussion about ethics (or orthopraxis), I want to clarify a few things. In this chapter I have discussed how the Western—or more specifically the White evangelical—church has traditionally viewed the study and preaching of doctrine from a primarily propositional framework. In the next chapter I will suggest that the African American church has traditionally viewed study and preaching from a primarily ethical framework.

I will be making large generalizations. There are many wonderful White and Black congregations where I have preached that practice a holistic Gospel. I think it is a reasonable assumption, based on observation, that among all racial and ethnic groups there have been some who have not taught or preached a theologically correct, biblical Gospel, as well as churches in all groups that have neither preached nor lived out biblical ethics.

All ethnic groups have had preachers and individuals who came to the realization that their particular religious experience was lacking and maybe not a truly biblical one, either doctrinally or ethically, and therefore have looked at other racial or ethnic groups as a place to find what was missing. Sometimes they have found it, and sometimes they have not.

My tradition, that of a conservative view of both the Bible and theology with its commitment to sound Bible and Gospel preaching, has sometimes been attractive to those who have missed it in their own traditions. It is certainly a tradition and practice that I am thankful for and wish everyone could enjoy, but it is only one side of a two-sided coin, and without the other side is incomplete. The words of Jesus show us what is essential: hearing his words and then putting his words into practice are both necessary.

I don't want to simply set up a contrast between White doctrinal understanding and Black ethical living, as if White people have the good doctrine and Black people teach the right way to live. My point is that there has been something missing in the way many White Christians have understood theology as opposed to the way African Americans have understood theology. What the great theological schools taught, what the conservative denominations believed and defended with tenacity, was a distorted or truncated view of the Christian faith. The great quote from Frederick Douglass sums it up:

> What I have said respecting religion, I mean strictly to apply to the slaveholding religion of this land, and with no possible reference to Christianity proper; for, between the Christianity of this land, and the Christianity of Christ, I recognized the widest possible difference.[1]

What I will be addressing is not simply the essential Christian struggle for all of us, which is to heed the words of Scripture that tell us to be not simply hearers of the Word, but doers also (Jas. 1:22–25). No, my emphasis has to do with the completeness of a theology that continues to leave out not only the ethical implications of the Gospel but the clear ethical commands of love, mercy, and brotherhood as the necessary good works that must become evident in our lives. This is manifested in the texts and subjects that most White pastors preach from and what they emphasize, and it is measurable if one were to look over a lifetime of preaching subjects.

The issues of race, slavery, injustice, poverty, and oppression that have been lived out in front of conservative, Reformed, and Evangelical Christians, and in which they sometimes had a hand in contributing to the evils of said injustice, makes you wonder what their theology had to say about such things. Did they have a different Bible, a different Christ, a different God? Did their prejudices and racism blind them to obvious evil, or was their theology deficient? What imprisoned them to preach with energy and venom against heresies rather than to be motivated from the truths of Scripture to *"... act justly and to love mercy and to walk humbly with your God"* (Mic. 6:8)?

Historic Presbyterianism has great examples of preachers calling for civil disobedience up to armed rebellion against what they saw as injustice. From John Knox to John Winthrop we see strident belief that without civil freedoms there is no freedom of faith, religion, or conscience. We see this echoed in African American Presbyterian preacher Henry Highland Garnet's speech to the delegates of the National Negro Convention in 1843, known as the "Call to Rebellion."[2]

The things that bind these Presbyterian preachers in their stand against injustice is an existential reality of injustice, or at least perceived injustice. Yet the White theological tradition has been to ignore what was happening to people of color in this nation, and when those Christians of color complained, the White conservative Christians rebuked them for their social justice activism.

It is the spiritual captivity of privilege to maintain the status quo and deny freedom—or the quest for freedom—to others, while glorying in their own historical stands for freedom from a British king or Union army.

May our right love of right doctrine be only one side of the theological coin. May we balance that necessary A-side of our theology with the equally necessary B-side. We turn to that lived-out B-side next.

---

1. Frederick Douglass, *Narrative of an American Slave*, Appendix, "http://utc.iath.virginia.edu/abolitn/abaufda14t.html"
2. Henry Highland Garnett, "An Address to the Slaves of the United States of America," in *Crossing the Danger Water: Three Hundred Years of African-American Writing*, ed. Deirdre Mullane, 115-121 (New York, NY: Anchor Books, 1993).

SUGGESTIONS

1. Read the next chapter, about B-side theology! Ask God to show you any cultural blindspots you have as you read and interpret God's Word.

2. Ask God to deepen your understanding of his Word. Review your preaching texts and subjects over the last few years (if you have been preaching that long). Or analyze the texts and subjects preached at your current church to see where they fall on the A-side/B-side spectrum.

PART THREE

ETHICS

EMBRACING B-SIDE THEOLOGY

As the body without the spirit is dead, so faith without deeds is dead.
James 2:26

So knowing and understanding the Word of God is certainly an important qualification for anyone in pastoral ministry. But in the Bible, knowing is never solely intellectual but also experiential. This brings us to what Dr. Carl Ellis calls B-side theology or what should be the ethical manifestation of our knowledge of God.

What do we do with what we have been shown and that which we have come to know? Micah 6:8 says: *"He has shown you, O man, what is good. And what does the Lord require of you? To act justly and to love mercy and to walk humbly with your God."*

Knowing is a starting place, but it can never be the finish. One of the greatest problems of Western, and especially American, Christianity is the failure to live out in our private and public lives what we know God wants of us. This of course has always been a challenge for any believer of any culture. As James wrote before there was such a country called America: *"Do not merely listen to the word, and so deceive yourselves. Do what it says"* (Jas. 1:22).

Some of us still don't know the discrepancy. We were taught Evangelical theology. We were taught that people need to be saved and that there is a creedal formula people need to believe in order to be saved. Some of us were taught that God wants holiness, but we were also taught that faith negates their lack of it, so they can still get into heaven without actually practicing any holiness. People claim to believe in eternal security (that we can't lose our salvation) as long as we have said the magic words, "Jesus, come into my heart."

AN INCOMPLETE GOSPEL

We have used this Evangelical theology to sometimes minimize our hypocrisy, and in the process we have actively worked against the credibility of the faith. Please bear with me, and don't be too quick to think that I am speaking against the necessity of faith or the grace God gives us in justification. I am for a biblical faith, but against a false kind of faith that uses phrases and simple prayers as a shallow substitute for the real thing.

One of the interesting things about Western, especially American, Christianity is the mixture of an extreme intellectualism in theological study with an irrational view of what it means to be a Christian. When I say irrational, I mean people thinking you can live any way you want to live and still go to heaven, so long as you have some historical moment in your life when you prayed the Sinner's Prayer. Or setting aside the hope of heaven, that you could claim to be a Christian but live completely opposite to the teaching and model of Jesus and still think anyone would take you seriously, especially God.

I am not merely speaking to the issue of how our personal lives need to reflect holiness to back up our confession of being saved by

Christ. I am speaking about a historic deficiency in the articulation of theology. There is danger in having an academic and propositional theology that places so much emphasis on getting doctrine (especially systematic theology) right but leaves out those doctrines that stress both the character and agenda of God when it comes to righteousness, especially social and corporate ethical righteousness. I speak here primarily of justice and mercy and the Kingdom of God.

As I further develop these thoughts, let me warn you that I will be attempting to explain the A-side/B-side dichotomy to some extent as I compare the formation of the White and the Black church in America. Please remember I am speaking in generalities. It is not my intent to make all White people feel bad, though sometimes it might be hard to avoid that. Nor do I want to paint a picture that the historic Black church has been divorced from sound propositional truth.

I am very thankful for those White churches and preachers who have stood not only for the doctrinally sound preaching of the cross, but also for living out the life of the cross in calling for justice in society, suffering with those who have been abused, and seeking a remedy for injustice through law and in relationships. We do have White heroes of justice in America, for whom I praise God. Unfortunately, in my understanding of American church history, too often these examples have been the exception and not the rule. This means that some of what I say will be an indictment of our Evangelical history.

Dr. Carl Ellis, when speaking of this A-side and B-side theology, refers to a generalized difference between the White American church and the Black church experience.[1] This difference has also been noted by many other theologians such as Dietrich Bonhoeffer, James W. McClendon Jr., as well as by James Cone and historian Jemar Tisby. As I mention any theologian, I am aware that our own theological convictions can cause us to become defensive at the mention of a name associated with views with which we do not agree. This becomes a problem when we stop listening to the truth, even when it comes from someone with whom we might disagree about other things.

I find it hard to listen to Southern theologians because they justified slavery, yet many of the things about which they wrote concerning biblical theology are still true. I despise the anti-semitism of Luther, yet love his understanding of salvation by grace through faith.[2] Therefore, in all things, let us be discerning.

---

1. See Carl F. Ellis, *Free at Last? The Gospel in the American Experience*, 2nd ed. (Downers Grove, IL: InterVarsity Press, 1996).
2. James W. McClendon, Jr., *Systematic Theology*, vol. 1, *Ethics* (Nashville, TN: Abingdon, 1986).

HISTORICAL CONTEXT

The Black church is a church born and formed by racial exclusion from the White majority—thus forcing and creating a racial solidarity (first among enslaved Africans and then among freed people), with a corresponding communal life forged by a struggle to survive, protect, believe in a loving God, rejoice and celebrate, and give hope to a suffering people. In contrast, the White American church took the comfort of God's blessing for granted. This is not to say White people knew or know nothing about suffering, but they have rarely faced that suffering as a people group. In fact, most White folks have not thought of themselves as a people group except in the deliberate hostility toward, opposition to, and exclusion of people of color.

The White church has had the luxury of allowing its members to think of themselves primarily as individuals. This is a self-identity born out of privilege, power, and materialism. Individual White Christians are encouraged to think of their personal moral behavior, the choices they make to do or not do the right thing.

The Black church, however, has been forced to deal with the broader and more extensive issue of ethics (the system that defines right and wrong not only for individuals but for society), because it sees its members as being under an existential threat. It is not simply the moral behavior of individuals about which the Black church is concerned (and certainly many Black preachers have been very concerned about the personal sins and moral life of their congregants and community), but the systemic moral culture in which all Americans live that creates, builds, and preserves injustice against people of color. It has been difficult for White preachers to speak against systemic injustice, let alone notice it, for many reasons. One is that they tend to look first for individuals to blame for the injustice.

It was the ethical system in America that allowed and perpetuated racism. It was the initial ethical system of colonial White America that had the audacity to deny people of color the right to be thought of or treated as individually possessing the *imago Dei* (image of God). White Christians might struggle with their personal honesty or personal lust, but they were allowed (or allowed others), without moral censure, to steal Africans from their home countries, enslave them, treat them as property, indulge in sexual immorality with them, rip apart their families for financial gain, exclude them from economic opportunity and personal friendship, and generally deprive them of life, liberty, and the pursuit of happiness.

The ethical system of early White Christian America allowed Whites to do these things to Black people without guilt or injury to their moral conscience. Even if Black folks were in fact people, some types of American Evangelical theology created a necessity for soul salvation without a corresponding necessity of physical or social justice. This allowed a context of no ethical responsibility for the preservation of Black existence. One of the great exceptions to this is the holistic ethical stand of Christian abolitionists before the Civil War.

Individualistic morality was focused on personal behavior, and churches saw this as their proper venue when it came to the

49

preaching of morals. As American history progressed, ethics in the public or social realm was increasingly interpreted by Evangelicals as politics, and thus many churches stayed out of it. Some resisted a public commitment to justice because it would have turned the system of White privilege upside-down. So they used theological constructs such as the "spirituality of the church" to maintain an unjust status quo.

White privilege was assumed as a corresponding benefit of White superiority, and it was reinforced by violence against any uprising or uppityness from Black folk, especially in the antebellum South. After the period of slavery, this commitment to White superiority and privilege continued not simply as an attitude. It continued through coordinated action (via heinous violence and terror) in the White Southern struggle against Reconstruction, through the days of Jim Crow laws and segregation, through the experience of economic oppression via sharecropping in the South, exclusion from labor unions in the North, and redlining of Black neighborhoods, along with racial housing covenants and exclusions.

The Black church could see the struggle of White Christians with their concern for personal morality as a cruel joke. White Christians spoke of the necessity to not lie, cheat, slander, steal, or live in a sexually immoral manner against their (White) neighbors. At the same time, they conducted politics, economics, and social relationships with a demonstrably non- and even anti-Christian testimony by refusing to see Black folks as neighbors. As Christians, they were supposed to love any and all human beings according to the Second Great Commandment and the words of Jesus.

This cruel history has been a perverse gift to the Black church, and therefore to the world, because it has protected the Black church from thinking of human beings simply as souls. The platonic philosophy of elevating the ideal and producing a distinction between the spiritual (good) and material (bad) buttressed a developing Western tradition of theological intellectual discourse divorced from the necessity of caring about the physical. This was a philosophical corruption that has largely been absent from the historic Black church.

The Black church has been forced to acknowledge the love God has for all of a human being, soul and body, because it was the bodies of Black folk that were at stake in the struggle against life-ending experiences such as lynching. This is one of the historic markers for the modern concept of Black Lives Matter. One aspect of the Christian religion—the White one—seems to convey the message: "No, your physical life in your body doesn't matter." The Black church firmly insists, by contrast, that the body (including Black bodies!) does indeed matter.

This means that how somebody treats another human being, or whole groups of people, speaks to the reality of his or her religion. One Gospel song says, "I'm gonna treat everybody right...." That is sort of an old idea when we look at James 1:27: *"Religion that God our Father accepts as pure and faultless is this: to look after orphans and widows in their distress and to keep oneself from being polluted by the world."* In this verse, ethics and morality are not simply keeping yourself from being polluted by the world, which is a very Christian desire, but also to help suffering people who are in distress. It is both and has always been both.

You cannot be true to the Scriptures unless you have not only a theological appreciation for justice and mercy, but a positive practice of them as well. In terms of pastoral competency, pastors are good leaders in their churches when they cast theological vision and provide biblical teaching about good works and what they consist of in the present context. More pointedly, the pastor must preach in practical terms as he calls his people to pursue godly obedience in a life of justice and mercy.

So while no church tradition has a lock on the market for getting everything right, there are realities that the historic Black church has faced that have forced it to speak consciously about the ethical or B-side of biblical theology. Whatever your church tradition, as a pastor it is imperative that you also be competent in teaching and doing the ethical aspects of being obedient to Christ.

This is where the rubber meets the road. Once a preacher identifies areas of sin, he takes a risk. Areas of sin are not simply personal moral issues. They are also societal, corporate, and economic issues. For example, when some pastors in the antebellum South spoke out against slavery, they lost their jobs and social connections as a result. Some put their own lives at risk by speaking out against the issue.

ETHICAL PREACHING

There are several challenges to understanding, preaching, and living out a biblical ethic for pastors. The first questions you must ask are: Will you and how will you preach against sin?

My tradition, the Reformed community, has had various approaches to preaching ethics and especially the Law. While the Westminster Confession and Catechisms emphasize a knowing of the Law, it is often used in a moralistic fashion and leans toward legalism and condemnation—which perversely some Reformed preachers think helps people see the need for repentance! The Westminster Larger Catechism is more detailed in its treatment of the Law and offers societal implications. One example of this would be the explanation of *"Thou shalt not steal,"* where it condemns "man-stealing," a pretty straightforward condemnation of the racial slave trade. Another attempt has been Christian Reconstructionism and Theonomy, which appeals for societal reformation on the basis of the Law, usually from a politically conservative agenda. Without a strong preaching of the Gospel and grace, all such uses of the Law become oppressive.

So as a pastor, you have some decisions to make. Will you

always speak generically against societal sin, hoping the Holy Spirit will bring personal application to each person's heart? Will you speak in a moralistic fashion, calling on people to do better in specific moral areas but offering them no hope in Gospel power or grace? Will you speak in a legalistic fashion, condemning and using guilt to manipulate?

The Gospel preacher knows (or should know) that he must explain the bad news to people about the reality of their own sin and sinfulness. This is unpleasant enough, but as long as he approaches it in a general way, no one can accuse him of being against something specific. But when you preach the Ten Commandments and get specific about kinds of sins, people may accuse you of being legalistic and judgmental. They may not get upset about you preaching against the "big sins," like murder and stealing, because we all expect preachers to be against those things. But when you start quoting Jesus warning against our negative heart attitudes, that's when people may say you've "gone to meddling."

When you take on issues where sin has been allowed to flourish, opposition likely will arise. If repentance means our racism must end, or our greed and materialism must diminish, or we must begin to treat our workers justly, or that any one of a number of behaviors must stop, then resistance might not be far off. Think of the riot in Ephesus by the silversmiths (Acts 19:23ff).

The risk is not just that some people might become angry because their privilege or position is threatened. You must also be discerning in what you say so as to be measured in your balance of prophetic preaching with Gospel forgiveness. There are many instances of injustice in the world. We can easily get caught up in a passionate campaign to end such injustice, especially if we have been affected or know those who have. Instead of being Gospel-driven we can become cause-oriented. Living for a cause can create tunnel vision, and we can forget to love those we oppose.

It takes wisdom and godly counsel to know where we ought to

stand. Sometimes the perpetrator of injustice has motives for which we should have some compassion. If nonbelievers only know us for what we are against, how can we attract them to a Savior who is able to change them, especially when they don't yet know change is necessary?

The political predisposition of people often accounts for how sympathetic, or unsympathetic, they are to sinners committing certain sins. For political conservatives, being against abortion seems to be the right thing, but how about the woman going to get the abortion? Does she need love, compassion, understanding, and a way out? How about the abortion doctors and nurses who make their living from the practice? Is there any avenue of love or on-ramp to repentance for them, or are they simply the enemy? Some passionate individuals have come to the conclusion that it is OK to kill such enemies. If there were ever an ethical challenge for Gospel preachers, it might show up right here.

The same struggle comes up over the LGBTQ+ identity group. Most conservative Christians believe that the Scriptures teach against the practice of same-gender sex. In fact, they believe it is not only a sin but a judgment. American cultural history reveals that this was a behavior that was not dealt with in a compassionate or understanding way in the past, but was simply condemned. There was plenty of condemnation, but hardly ever any call for repentance, let alone forgiveness or reconciliation, for those who practiced it. This was true not only for Evangelicals but for the nation as a whole.

In today's climate, some Gospel preachers refuse to condemn homosexual practice as a sin in order to create an atmosphere of welcome while still calling people to faith and conversion. They soft-pedal a stance against the sin because they seem to want to make up for the sins of society against gay people. Other pastors think that even the tendency toward same-sex attraction is sinful, and therefore they could never make room in their congregations for someone who has this struggle.

Gospel preaching in areas of moral behavior is not simply therapy to help victims of their own sin feel better about the things that bind them and enslave them. It is the preaching of liberation, deliverance, and forgiveness! It is the preaching of a new identity in our union with Christ in spite of the struggles we have. There are millions of people in great angst over devastated sexual identities, and more millions in perpetual emotional desperation over dominating self-wickedness. In answer to these morally conscience-stricken populations, we have some preachers attempting to rewrite what sin is and is not so as not to cause offense. This is the same as thinking that a cancer diagnosis is the problem instead of the cancer itself.

MORAL COURAGE

Moral courage is necessary to take an ethical stand and preach an ethical challenge. You must fear God rather than man, and you must have faith that God loves you and you are safe in him, no matter what opposition may arise.

How do we discern the ethical stand on any particular matter? Does God hate sin or not, and does he or does he not call us to hate evil? Proverbs 8:13 says, *"To fear the Lord is to hate evil."* Are we able in this present day to declare anything as evil, except of course an attitude of intolerance? Each generation faces moments that challenge its moral courage. There will always be the biblical standard to hate evil, to call sin what it is—*sin*—and to let people know that God hates it. Sin is a transgression against God's law. It is not just a failure to meet the standard, born of weakness, but also an act of rebellion against what God has declared he wants from us. By mentioning particular sins you may create hurt, guilt, shame, and sometimes isolation for those caught up in it. But only an awareness of such sin can lead to repentance.

Fundamentalist churches used to condemn divorce, and it didn't seem to matter whether you were the innocent or guilty party in the divorce. If you were divorced, you were a failure, could not become a church officer, and might not be allowed to be a member. I remember once preaching from the text in Malachi 2:16 about how the Lord hates divorce. So when a couple in my congregation, who had been remarried after each had divorced their previous spouse, heard my reading and preaching on this text, they felt terrible and were a bit angry at me.

My conclusion about this verse is not that God hated that couple as individuals or a couple, nor that they stood condemned. Both had divorced as innocent parties. They had been sinned against. Even if they had committed adultery, my conviction was that they could be forgiven if they had repented and (through faith) been washed in their conscience by the blood of Christ. This is the atonement we Bible-believers love to hear and sing about. Yet my simple reading of the passage stirred feelings of regret in them.

When I know my church members are sensitive toward such issues, and when I happen to like those members or might be afraid they will get mad and take their tithe money and energies elsewhere, I might become shy about preaching on those topics. I might choose not to be so passionate against certain things. These are moments of temptation for pastors who would otherwise preach vigorously against sin, evil, and injustice.

So if I think abortion is the killing of an innocent child, homosexual practice is sin, and divorce is something God hates, will I then be able to say those things without hurting someone's feelings and driving them away from the church? It is almost impossible in our current culture to say something negative about any behavior without making someone feel guilty or angry. My answer is that if we are truly preaching a Gospel of grace and mercy, we can and must preach strongly against sin while simultaneously offering hope, healing, cleansing, conversion, change, victory, and forgiveness.

I cannot guarantee that people's feelings will not be hurt. It is inevitable that when you are against something and speak against it, then those who have experienced it, or practice it, or accept it, or believe in it will tend to resist your message. Unless the Holy Spirit is working repentance in them, they very well might turn against you. This is a potential cost of ethical preaching.

The pastor who preaches against sin and for holiness must certainly check his own attitude. Are your temperament and preaching characterized by love, mercy, understanding, and reconciliation? Living in a relativistic culture which has very few absolutes (except believing that there are no moral absolutes) makes it hard to take clear moral stands. Some preachers wait until the collective culture is in agreement before speaking about an issue. History shows that culture often changes and so does its moral standard. In my opinion, slavery was always wrong, but it wasn't always thought to be so, especially as it seemed to be justified by a world whose history was built on slavery in many contexts.

All the ethical-moral strategies to deliver modernism from relativism have failed. Modernism cut us off from accepting revealed truth so we have tried Sentiment (Hume), Rationalism and Moral Imperatives (Kant), Utilitarianism (Bentham), and Social Contract Theory (Hobbs and Rawls).[1] Yet God has spoken, and it is the only thing that protects us from the drift inherent in modern moral philosophy.

In each generation Christians must read the Bible honestly and their culture self-critically. As they realize the contrast between God's standard and human behavior, they must preach God's Word, in spite of the current cultural climate, come hell or high water. It is what biblical courage requires, and it is what eventually changes culture as the moral conscience of the people is affected.

This is not an excuse for preachers to be mean-spirited or self-righteous. We are always to have the compassion and love of Jesus, no matter how nasty or messed up people might be. We need to remember the words of Jude: *"Be merciful to those who doubt; save others by snatching them from the fire; to others show mercy, mixed with fear—hating even the clothing stained by corrupted flesh"* (verses 22–23).

For those in the Reformed tradition, where doctrine and propositional theology play such a huge part in credentialing individual preachers (and therefore play a significant role in our choice of what to study, preach, and defend), we must face the question: Has our theology been adequate? If we have primarily focused on the propositional and rational aspects of our faith, and if we have sought to be always correct, quick to point out theological error, and tenacious in our defense of what is biblical, then what explains our failure to be biblically holistic in our teaching about ethics? What explains our failure to be faithful in living out that ethical and moral teaching?

---

1. Robert Kraft, University of Texas, "Quest for Meaning" lectures, The Teaching Company.

A MORE COMPLETE GOSPEL

I am not advocating a social Gospel rather than a biblical one. Nor am I redefining the Gospel. I am not attempting to change the theology of salvation, or the order in which God brings it about (Rom. 8:29–30), or the definition of justification, or the teaching of salvation by grace. I stand with the Reformers in all these things. But unfortunately the cry of hypocrisy against us by modern liberal critics is often correct, and we dare not let the failure of others to be faithful to the authority of Scripture assuage our guilt for being unfaithful in our application of the Scriptures.

I ask again, what explains the discrepancy? Is it the theology itself? Why do we seem to pick and choose what is important in the Word and endanger our own souls by despising our neighbors, the poor, and those who are oppressed (Matt. 25:31–46)? Oh how we wish, pray, and hope for preachers who know the Scriptures, the Law of God, good from bad theology, and how important and life-giving correct theology is for human beings. But this by itself is not good enough.

At the same time, and in the same persons, we also wish for

those who grasp how important it is to know, believe, preach, and live the *"more important matters of the law"* (Matt. 23:23). Oh for more preachers who know what is important to God and what ways of living absolutely reflect his character and attributes—love, mercy, and justice! We need to stop swallowing camels while we strain out gnats (Matt. 23:24).

I believe Reformed theology, as summarized in the Westminster Confession and Catechisms, is robust. I ascribe to the system of doctrine it teaches because I am in agreement with it. Yet I don't think it can be a completely adequate theology, simply because it fails to capture all that the Bible teaches. There are questions the Bible answers that the Confession does not, and one reason for that is the cultural context of the documents. There are questions which the authors of those documents were not asking but which our culture is asking, so the task of reforming our theology continues.

You can't find a geographical place to minster that doesn't have some challenge for the local church in its racial, ethnic, or economic history. We deal with either historical or present conflict. Our very lack of being cross-culturally missional becomes an ethical problem and reflects our cultural, and perhaps racial, bias. These are not simply social or political issues for each culture. They are also spiritual, missional, and ethical issues for the church.

Our tendency to gather only people in the same ethnic or socioeconomic group, and our fear of and resistance to welcoming the poor into our middle-class group, reveals our failure to obey Jesus' commission to preach the Gospel to the poor (Luke 4:16–21). Some refuse to share the Gospel with those different from themselves. Some will preach the Gospel to different races but then refuse to welcome them into their churches and disciple them. Both refusals are a disgrace and shame to the Bride of Christ, which is supposed to be made up of people who love.

Our faithfulness in following Jesus in reconciliation and showing merciful love to others reveals that, truly, the Father has sent him. We thus show we are his disciples as Jesus prayed (and revealed) in John 17:23: *"I in them and you in me—so that they may be brought to complete unity. Then the world will know that you sent me and have loved them even as you have loved me."* And then again in John 13:35: *"By this everyone will know that you are my disciples, if you love one another."*

On the other hand, our refusal to love and accept others different from ourselves, or our mistreatment of them, reveals something else about us: *"We love because he first loved us. Whoever claims to love God yet hates a brother or sister is a liar. For whoever does not love their brother and sister, whom they have seen, cannot love God, whom they have not seen"* (1 John 4:19–20). We are exposed as hypocrites, revealed as people who don't really love God.

Many White preachers have no idea that their preaching and living are out of balance. Their group ignorance is a symptom of their privilege. Black people can hardly conceive that this ignorance is anything but willful and a sign of a racist decision. Surely if White preachers pastored churches of people whose lives were at stake, whose members could not get a decent education, couldn't get jobs, couldn't get loans, couldn't get health care, felt oppressed by police and government authorities, and woke up to see their houses on fire or their churches being bombed, then they would think the Bible had something to say about such evil. But racism kills empathy, among other things.

So you see that the two sides of theology, the propositional A-side and the ethical B-side are both essential for the Gospel preacher. The competent pastor must know and do both. It is not enough to believe the right things. You need to live them out to show that your faith is real. Our fruit proves what kind of trees we are.

To be a Christian, it is not enough to believe the right things; you have to do them. We cannot say we love God—who we cannot see—if we won't love our brothers and sisters—who we can see. Likewise, you cannot be a sufficient pastor if you preach doctrine but don't teach how it applies to life, especially in the areas of justice and mercy. You must preach *and* live these truths for the complete Gospel to be presented, for God's glory.

SUGGESTIONS

I1. f you haven't done some kind of cultural and historical study of your context of ministry, I encourage you to start one now. This would include an ethnic and cultural history as well as a demographic study.

2. Ask several people of a different ethnicity than yourself in your church or neighborhood for their stories (their ethnographies). Start with some longtime residents of your area.

3. Pick out some books about the ethnic or cultural struggle of the people to whom you minister and find someone or a group with whom you can discuss it.

4.

Articulate the economic and justice issues the people of your church and neighborhood are facing. Are they the same? Are they in conflict? Are you or is anyone in your congregation doing or saying anything about these justice issues?

PART FOUR
PREACHING & TEACHING
MINISTERING THE WORD OF GOD

"And you will know that I have sent you this warning so that my covenant with Levi may continue," says the Lord Almighty. "My covenant was with him, a covenant of life and peace, and I gave them to him; this called for reverence and he revered me and stood in awe of my name. True instruction was in his mouth and nothing false was found on his lips. He walked with me in peace and uprightness, and turned many from sin. For the lips of a priest ought to preserve knowledge, because he is the messenger of the Lord Almighty and people seek instruction from his mouth."
Malachi 2:4–7

As pastors, we are entrusted with the Word of God and, as the priests were reminded by Malachi, to instruct with truth to turn many from sin. When we preach, teach, and instruct, we are to remember we are speaking the very words of God, and we are to serve in his strength, not ours. It is both a reassurance and a warning that we might be prone to attempt to do God's work without God's help.

If you are a pastor of a local church, preaching and teaching the

Word of God to your flock is your most essential task. In your daily reality you likely will face many distractions from this main focus. In this section I intend to delineate a lot of subtasks that make up the work of a pastor. None of us will be an expert on every subtask, and as I speak to them you may very well realize your inadequacy, as I certainly do.

Pastors are to be people of The Book. They are to know God and his Word, and they are to be ready to preach *"in season and out of season"* (2 Tim. 4:2). Yet even their preaching is something that should get better with experience, especially if their sermons are debriefed with loving encouragement. There are those who are saved and then called to the ministry in a very short space of time. They have had no experience in a church and have not been mentored by a pastor. These men especially need internships or apprenticeships to gain practical experience. They need to seek by all means to hone their skills.

PREACHING

Preach the word; be prepared in season and out of season....
2 Timothy 4:2

I lean toward the dramatic, especially when I preach to children. I try to use drama through stories, humor, passionate speech, and sometimes outrageous phrases or comments. Since the time I was first asked to speak about Jesus publicly beyond that of a simple testimony (in open air meetings), I have tried to hold the attention of people when I speak. Preaching in the open air means people don't owe you anything, not even the time of day. To hold their attention you must capture them, and I had to learn to do it with my voice, a story, an illustration, or some kind of argument they wanted answered. This fear of losing a crowd has helped me immensely in my preaching.

My conviction is that preaching is the primary tool in the pastor's box for helping people grow in their love for and commitment to Christ. It has always been the focus for the gathering and strengthening of the church. God decided that he was *"... pleased through the foolishness of what was preached to save those who believe"* (1 Cor. 1:21). In the same chapter, Paul tells us that he was not sent *"to baptize, but to preach the gospel"* (1 Cor. 1:17).

I wish I were a better preacher—more incisive, more prophetic, more biblical, and simply more effective in touching the hearts of men and women. In other words, this is another area in which I often feel insufficient.

I love to preach, and I love to see it affecting the people in the congregation. I don't know if anything else in my life has made me feel so worthwhile or useful for the Kingdom of God. Whenever I am complimented or praised for my preaching, I immediately seek to give glory to God. I am conscious that preaching (both doing it and listening to it) is a spiritual experience. I am aware that preaching is a gift God has given me, and when it goes well, I want to give the glory to him. I am blessed when he sees fit to use me in preaching. But when we preach, we must make sure that what is happening is more about Christ than about us.

As a pastor, learn how to prepare a sermon from those who have gone before you. My seminary homiletics professor, Dr. Robert G. Rayburn, gave me a strong foundation. I also benefited from lessons shared in books by Dr. Bryan Chapell, a fellow alumnus who later became president of Covenant Seminary.[1]

Reading and listening to sermons from gifted preachers can help you improve as well. In seminary, my wife would let me read to her sermons by Charles Spurgeon when we went on picnics. Listening to men such as Billy Graham, Tom Skinner, John Stott, and John Perkins has taught me much about communication and preaching.

Not everyone believes preaching is essential. Some think the sacrament of communion is what really holds the church together. Some pastors seem to resent the necessity of the pulpit, while for others it is an emotional and intellectual burden. I believe the Reformation recaptured the power of the early church in the importance of the preached Word as an opportunity for people to hear the Word of God taught with conviction and application.

There are abuses to the power inherent in the preaching pulpit. Preachers with charisma who preach heresy or manipulate their listeners have deceived many and caused great harm. Bad sermons, boring sermons, sermons that fail to engage or call for response, and irrelevant sermons all cause harm. Poor preaching trains people to assume that sermons are simply to be endured and anesthetizes them to the piercing of their spiritual hearts by truth. Every bad sermon works against a pastor's efforts to keep people coming back to church.

Good preaching from pastors of integrity, especially over significant periods of time, can result in great spiritual depth for both individual believers and the church as a whole. Good preaching is preventative counseling. Good preaching can accomplish spiritual change in a moment of time within a heart that has been resisting God for years. Good preaching attracts people and holds churches together while bad preaching drives folks away. If you are going to be a pastor, you should strive to be a great preacher. Even if you never achieve it, you should at least aim for it.

Powerful sermons—sermons that are used by God in the minds and hearts of people to bring conviction, repentance, and change— don't necessarily have to shine with academic brilliance. Powerful sermons don't have to be full of quotes, nor do they have to reference great commentaries. But truly great sermons do need to be biblical. There have been plenty of preachers with notable oratorical skills, whose intellectual brilliance and theological acumen have been delightfully displayed, yet have failed to preach from the Bible and thus failed to preach truth. This kind of preaching may be entertaining, but it is not true preaching, only a type of show business.

Sermons should be full of biblical truth, intellectually engaging, and memorable due to relevant quotes. It's fantastic when sermons cite history, use vivid illustration with the right touch of humor, hit relevant and contemporary issues of both society and the human heart. I am convicted when the preacher uses voice and timing with skill and then unleashes the important stab of personal application. Lord, give us more! Believers long for Spirit-filled preaching.

I encourage strong and adequate preparation. I heartily endorse the work and discipline that it requires, yet not all of our preparation habits are the same. The question is: What really prepares you? If hours in commentaries doesn't make your sermons better, then maybe you need a different approach.

I am not recommending an anti-intellectual kind of preaching. Since sermons are by their very nature intellectual and use language, the listeners must be able to understand and follow the stories, logic, and arguments presented by the preacher. This requires prior thought on the part of the preacher. Some preachers are quick at grasping the logical argument inherent to the text, while others must struggle through it. Don't confuse length of study with adequate preparation. Sometimes great amounts of time in study are actually the indulgence of an introverted academic and not the stoking of a fire to be unleashed.

Some preaching is not very logical. Some sermons are bare emotional outbursts and not easily deciphered. Some preachers and congregations seek to have a preaching experience that is as mystical and emotional as possible. While such sermons might appeal to some and even be moving, they are ultimately unhelpful if they fail to present God's truth rather than someone's personal view of truth. My point is that those sermons with no logic or argument and which lack a presentation of biblical truth are bad sermons.

At the same time, sermons that contain or display no emotion, which fail to speak to the human heart but are mere academic lectures, that simply recite truths or theological observations from a text and give no application, these also are bad sermons. Some have been raised on this kind of academic preaching and seem terrified by emotion. They prefer a dry and impersonal recitation of truth. We understand that God is able to use his Word to bring about a changed heart, in whatever form it is delivered, but the preacher should not surrender to this woeful excuse for preaching. Sermons should always call for a response, and that response needs to be holistic—touching intellect, emotion, and volition.

In my experience as a pastor of a cross-cultural church, I have enjoyed exposure to many different preaching styles. I have enjoyed White (Anglo-European), African American, and African preachers. It is a joy to know men who love the Lord Jesus, are faithful in preaching from Scripture as though they believe it, and who deliver some fine sermons.

There are varying degrees of skill within any ethnic group when it comes to preaching. I have heard poor sermons from both Black and White preachers. Some were not being scriptural, and some were delivered poorly. Yet it is fair to generally say there is a Black style of preaching, and there is a White one.

The first Black preacher I remember hearing was Rev. Tom Skinner or, as he was also known, Evangelist Tom Skinner from Harlem. Listening to Tom was an experience. It was dramatic, and it was forceful. As he preached, he made an argument that caught you up and then carried you to the conclusion. His stature, voice, grasp of societal facts, humor, illustrations, rhetorical questions, and points of application kept me enthralled. He had great timing, and he knew how to use various smiles and grimaces. He had a spiritual and social righteousness agenda. It was hard to leave his sermons without thinking you were now responsible to do something about it.

I have listened to many other wonderful Black preachers, and I suggest that you find and listen to recordings of such men as EV Hill, Gardner Taylor, Elder Ward, and even TD Jakes (as far as preaching style is concerned but not for orthodox truth). There is drama in the good preachers, great storytelling, often a sense of humor, and the use of anecdotes and illustrations to make powerful points. In African American preaching you can hear this rhythm and cadence, a sense of timing, as if the sermon is being sung. You can hear this cadence when you listen to sermons by Dr. Martin

Luther King Jr. Some preachers even end their sermons with "hooping" or singing their closing thoughts. The best ones make sense doing it, while others just seem to make sounds while the Hammond B3 organ keeps the beat.

Some church folk feel like they haven't had church unless the preacher hoops and people get happy and start shouting and fainting. I went to a choir concert once in a Black church where half the choir fainted during a song, then the nurses who went to help them started fainting. Somehow or other we all got to the end of the song, but it was something to watch. Black preaching and the Black worship experience is often more emotional than White preaching.

Pentecostal preaching is a little different, as it sometimes is affected preaching with certain common phrases or grunts repeated often to give a sense of emotion. It is a learned style of preaching. Obviously any style can be affected or phony, and almost any style can be sincere and Spirit-empowered. Great Black preachers have had an intuitive sense of the art of preaching, knowing how to use the intellectual elements while fleshing out a story with passion in their deliveries.

I only call a preacher a good one (of any ethnic group or culture) if he stays true to the Word of God. If he invents his own ideas or application apart from biblical truth, then it doesn't matter how skillful an orator he is. Once a preacher loses touch with what the Bible is saying, he is no longer a good preacher.

Some White preachers seem to be almost scientific in their approach as they attempt to be academic and appeal to the cognitive side of the brain. They might build an exegetical argument, sometimes going line by line, explaining words, tenses, and translation. It is often like listening to a lecture. Some White preachers are very good at illustrations and at connecting points of Scripture that didn't seem obvious at first.

Really good preachers find appropriate quotes from exceptional or intriguing people, possibly using some facts or data from the social sciences, which seems to give them a double authority. Using popular culture references can help carry a point. However pop culture references are not equally appreciated or understood by all people, which can be a problem. White preachers tend to be more historical, citing church councils, creeds, and Reformers, as if the past were more important than the present. Black preachers tend to be better at anecdotal, metaphorical storytelling.

God saves people and blesses people through all kinds of preachers, no matter their ethnicity. Black preachers often feel free to make social or ethical commentary with current application, and the history of their people seems to give them the moral weight to make those comments. I have learned much from all kinds of preaching.

I absolutely love a good sermon in which I am terribly convicted by God, or feel filled with God, or that draws me to greater faith. Great sermons or even wonderful and salient points in average sermons have changed the course of my life, given me hope on some very dark days, brought insight and conviction about my own sins, and taught me much about God. Our churches need pastors full of God, and they need great preaching. There is no substitute for this. May the Lord help you to be a preacher who can stand and deliver, who can bring it, in Spirit and in Truth.

As we go out with the Gospel, we also want the Gospel to be clearly and boldly shared in our worship. One of my elders told me he got saved when he heard the call to worship and then the Scripture text read before my sermon. That is Holy Ghost work, sure enough. We pray and hope for people to be saved in our worship and through our preaching. Pastors need to learn how to weave the Gospel story in and through their sermons, both for the lost to hear it and understand it, and also to keep preaching it to believers so they can be reminded of their salvation, justification, and adoption.

We do not assume Sunday morning is sufficient for evangelizing the lost. Most of the lost don't ever come to church, but when they do they ought to be able to hear the Gospel so that they can understand it. Please understand that when I say "weave the

Gospel" I don't mean just using the word "Gospel" but articulating what it is, how it is Good News, what Christ did on the cross. Too many so-called grace churches use the words "grace" and "Gospel" a lot, but they fail to preach the Gospel.

---

1. Bryan Chapell, *Christ-Centered Preaching: Redeeming the Expository Sermon*, 3rd ed. (Baker Academic, 2018); *Christ-Centered Sermons: Models of Redemptive Preaching* (Baker Academic, 2013); *Using Illustrations to Preach with Power*,(Wheaton, IL: Crossway, 2001).

WORSHIP

For the director of music. To the tune of "Lilies,"
Of the Sons of Koah. A maskil. A wedding song.
—Instructions prior to Psalm 45

We may hear criticisms of worship practices as entertainment.
People may say that our worship has one audience, and that is the
Lord God—he is the one we are to please and to bless. However,
every person involved in public worship has to perform. If you
noticed the phrase that began this chapter (from Psalm 45), it shows
us worship was produced. There were directions given as to which
tune to use. Worship requires both planning and participation.
Preachers perform, readers of Scripture or liturgists perform, those
who pray perform, singers perform, and even ushers perform. If
you move, speak, or do anything physical in a worship service, you
are performing. I am not against performing in this sense. What I
want is for you to perform this worship well, with skill, and all for
the glory of God, and not for yourself or your own aggrandizement.
Preachers need to understand this, as they are the main performers
in worship services.

As I read the Bible, I realize that worship is not simply an activity meant for one day of the week. I believe it is the reason we exist, the strength and joy of our lives, and our future. As the book of Psalms comes to a close, the last words are, *"Let everything that has breath praise the Lord. Praise the Lord"* (Ps. 150:6).

I enjoy Psalm 148 too. It goes through a roll call of creation and humanity and invites all parts of the world and humans from every station to praise the Lord. I enjoy singing the words of this psalm whenever we sing, "Hallelujah, Praise Jehovah."

Why is worship such a big deal? The short answer is—God! God is not a metaphysical concept; he is a person. God is the supreme personality of the universe and the most intimate of beings. He is the reason everything exists, and he is the ultimate purpose of everything. There is no sense, logic, or organization to being, life, history, or existence without him.

Without him there is no joy, and in his presence there is fullness of joy (Psalm 16). Worship means we are happy—happy in him, happy with him, satisfied, content, and thankful for all that he is and has been in our lives. Without joy in worship, there is not much worship at all! God is to be feared; he is omnipotent and therefore awesome. As the one who can not only kill you but after doing that is able to cast your soul into hell, he ought to be feared (Matt. 10:28). He is holy, and the realization of his holiness leaves us undone (Isa. 6). He never does anything wrong, and there is no corruption or evil within him.

But fear and dread are not in themselves sufficient for worship. God is knowable, and he seeks to be known. For us to know God and to be known by him is what it means to be fully loved. The Bible teaches us that God seeks worshipers, so worship is what he wants. But he insists that we worship him *"in the Spirit and in truth"* (John 4:23).

God reveals himself generally through creation, but he reveals himself in a special way in the Bible. To focus on one story, one incident, or one aspect of God and not put the pieces together as he presents himself in the full biblical revelation means we will have a truncated view of God. There are scary parts in the Bible, where we realize that this God is not be treated lightly. He has laws, and he enforces them. Yet all through the Bible, the people who draw close to God love him and are loved by him. They are happy in him, joyful in him, and blessed in him.

The existence of God calls for a response from an aware creation and from aware creatures. Unaware creatures (and here I speak of human beings who are dead in their sins and as yet unable to discern spiritual things) still carry in themselves a loss, a vacuum, a hole that only God can fill. When the Holy Spirit brings a spiritually dead person to new life, that hole is filled. When we become spiritually alive, we finally get to fellowship with the supreme spiritual being of the universe!

Part of our worship is the joy that comes from the acknowledgment that through Jesus Christ we can know God. Jesus came into the world so that we might know God, that we might have eternal life, and that we might have his joy fulfilled in us (John 17). Our knowledge of God and fellowship with him can only come through God's work of grace which provides a solution for the things that alienated us from our Creator in the first place. Our sins have separated us from his fellowship, broken us, and brought death into the world. Sin and death have to be dealt with before we can enjoy a relationship with God, and that is exactly what God provided for us in Jesus when he died on the cross and rose again from the dead.

Jesus calls us his friends (John 15:15). We are called joint-heirs with Christ (Rom 8:17), and we are called children of God (1 John 3:1). This is intimate fellowship, a familial relationship, and the testimony of this work of God in our lives ought to continually fill us with gratitude, joy, and praise. We have reasons to worship!

Christians ought to approach worship as a duty dearly sought, enjoyed, and as something we become quite miserable without. Our hearts ought to yearn to be in the courts of the Lord: *"How lovely is your dwelling place, Lord Almighty! My soul yearns, even* faints, for the courts of the Lord; my heart and my flesh cry out for the living God" (Ps. 84:1–2). Do you want God that much when you go to church, when you anticipate what it means to worship with the people of God? It is a shame that many have never had that kind of church worship experience, and there is no reason this should be so, not if our pastors create joyful and wonderful worship services.

For it is our pleasure and great privilege to come into God's presence. We are to be moved when we come into worship. Worship calls for an emotional response of praise, singing, testimony, rejoicing, and thanks. All of these are part of the offerings we bring to God. God's truth—the Scriptures—guide us in the intellectual and cognitive content of which we sing and speak.

We are not to come in our arrogance, complacency, or ignorance. We are always learning in our worship. We learn more about God and our desperate need for him. Worship was not given to us by God as something that can only be enjoyed by the thoroughly theologically trained, but he does demand that we take him seriously and come to him in a balance of fearful respect and ecstatic joy.

As Paul puts it in Ephesians 3:17–19:

> And I pray that you, being rooted and established in love, may have power, together with all the Lord's holy people, to grasp how wide and long and high and deep is the love of Christ, and to know this love that surpasses knowledge—that you may be filled to the measure of all the fullness of God.

There is a danger in making the worship of God so intellectual that it becomes unreachable by the common person. One night I went to an evening worship service at a sister congregation that has more of a high church feel to their worship. Their music department was performing worship music, and they were doing a very good job of it. They also had some reflections on the music by their director of worship. He made comments that implied we could not worship adequately unless we could discern the layers of Bach's music that taught about the Holy Trinity through his use of musical technique.

I later told their pastor that I thought such comments were as close to heresy as I had heard in one of our churches. I appreciate Bach, or at least I feel blessed to hear his work, and I am moved and impressed by it. But I cannot discern all of his techniques as I simply don't have the musical training and aptitude. So where does that leave those of us who are "unprepared to worship adequately," as we listen to Bach? The statement was ridiculous and certainly has no biblical basis. Worship is for everyone, and even rocks get to do it if people fail to praise the Lord (Luke 19:40).

If you are the pastor, then you are responsible for the planning and conduct of the worship service. You should wish to never have this responsibility taken away from you, although you might choose to delegate its planning to your chief musician. You will always be responsible as to whether or not the worship service is God-honoring, approachable, understandable by the people, and faithful to Scripture. For a short time, we allowed our ushers to say the offertory prayer prior to their collection. One time the ushers allowed a young volunteer to pray. When we realized she was praying to her deceased mother we knew we needed to step up our oversight!

If you frighten your elders with rash or strange changes to the order of worship, they may wish to take this authority away from you, so make sure you are consulting with them. Train them in understanding and accomplishing your vision (hopefully a shared one) in the development of worship, especially in regard to culture. Keep their confidence by dealing with disruptions, unintended heresy, and poor performance on the part of worship and song leaders, Scripture readers, and even aspiring preachers.

We have a principle of worship in the Presbyterian church called the Regulative Principle. It helps us stay faithful to Scripture in our corporate worship as the Body of Christ. Essentially, we don't insert "strange fire" or idol worship into a church service by coming up with new ideas or innovative practices that aren't taught in the Bible (Lev. 10:1).

Pastor Derek Thomas quotes John Calvin as saying, "God disapproves of all modes of worship not expressly sanctioned by his Word."[1] We try to be faithful to the commandments in how we worship (Ex. 20:2–6). However it is important to remember that all worship services happen in a cultural context. It is easy to think we are conducting biblical worship when it is actually a cultural form of worship to which we have become accustomed. In America most every worship service is a cultural hybrid of some sort.

How is proper Presbyterian worship cultural and not simply theological in its presentation? People worship in language, and each language is part of a culture. Worship is conducted with words, thoughts, feelings, and actions. Worship as described in the psalms is far more physical and emotive than is usually seen in American Presbyterianism. For some African Americans, saying "Amen" out loud is taken for granted and is often simply the beginning of a running dialogue with the preacher or a commentary as the preacher preaches.

I have actually heard Presbyterians say, "We are saying amen in our hearts" or "We are bowing in our hearts," while they are not actually saying anything out loud or physically bowing. I have been in worship services where almost any vocal utterance or physical response (such as clapping) was forbidden. I just wonder what the writer of the Psalms would have thought about that!

Many of the worship wars people fight are really about cultural choices and not theology. Which instruments should be used? How loud should the music be? Can we move, raise our hands, dance, shout, clap—or is that bad or even sinful because it distracts others?

Which aspects of your preferred liturgy are actually biblically directed or simply what you think is desirable? Robes, kneeling, candles, responsive readings, written prayers, and corporate confessions are prescribed for us in which biblical passages? Having people give spontaneous responses or verbally contributing to worship without pastoral approval is described where in Scripture? How much of the planning of your worship is really a current fad or church-growth idea, and what is definitely Bible-commanded or Bible-modeled?

Yes, we have a Reformed tradition, and it can teach us much. Some of it came about as a reaction to practices that were not biblical. We have some sources that tell us how the early church worshiped, especially from something called the Didache or the teaching.[2] This is one of the earliest (second century) known descriptions of the liturgy of the early church. Tradition, however, is not our standard. "Our only infallible rule of faith and practice is the Word of God," as says the Westminster Shorter Catechism.

I appreciate people having cultural preferences. I understand a pastor might think his preferred way of worshiping is biblical or the most helpful for his congregation. Some pastors are simply culturally ignorant, even of their own culture, in thinking their way is *the* way to worship, while labeling other cultural choices as unrighteous. We need to be biblical in all of our worship choices, and I think it is healthy for pastors and elders to be able to tell their people "this particular practice is not actually commanded, but is traditional, and we do it because...."

In the Presbyterian, Reformed, and Evangelical tradition, we believe in celebrating the sacraments, though we certainly debate how they are to be administered.

We believe in singing, though there are arguments as to what is appropriate to sing and then how to sing it. Should we only sing psalms? Can we sing them with a jazz or gospel rhythm, or must they be done like the Scots used to sing it? Oh, isn't that cultural? Should we sing as a congregation, and who should lead? Should the pastor or an elder lead the singing, or can a woman do it? Should we ever have a praise team or choir, and if so can we dress them in robes, or should we hide them in the back so no one sees them?

The point I am trying to make is that worship is something we create, shape, and perform, and it has cultural origins and implications. We must be careful not to take our cultures and simply baptize them with spirituality, nor attempt to do something which is impossible, which is to take worship out of culture. We are to be a biblical, God-focused, Christ-honoring people engaging holistically with understanding.

Presbyterians have had church schisms over psalm-singing and the use of instruments. My denomination doesn't demand a psalms-only worship without instruments. Then we have to debate which instruments are allowed which involves other cultural choices, for just where is the pipe organ listed in Scripture? It is strange how some hate to have an instrumentalist or soloist improvise and perform in a contemporary service, yet at a more traditional service they rejoice as some organist goes off the chain, flying up and down the pedals and keys. I have read that Calvin hated the tambourine, even though Miriam used it to lead Israel in worship. I love Calvin's theology, but I don't agree with him about the tambourine (except when someone plays it who has no rhythm).

---

1. Derek WH Thomas, "The Regulative Principle: Responding to Recent Criticism," *in Give Praise to God: A Vision for Reforming Worship: Celebrating the Legacy of James Montgomery Boice*, eds. Philip Graham Ryken, Derek WH Thomas, J LigonDuncan, III (Phillipsburg, NJ: P&R Publishing, 2003), 76.

2. For a translation and background information, see Thomas O'Loughlin, *The Didache: A Window on the Earliest Christians* (Grand Rapids, MI: Baker Academic, 2010).

SACRAMENTS

Do this in remembrance of me.
1 Corinthians 11:24

One great responsibility of and blessed opportunity for pastors is the administration of the sacraments. In the Protestant church we have two sacraments, baptism and the Lord's Supper, which is also called Holy Communion or the Eucharist. These are, or ought to be, precious moments in the life of the believer and the church. Far too often they are merely perfunctory when administered by pastors.

I won't attempt a full discussion of the theology of each sacrament here, but I do want to make a few points I hope will help you be more proficient in the way you administer them. By proficiently administering them, I mean that you make them Gospel events and give them the spiritual gravitas I believe Scripture gives them.

As a Reformed and covenantal believer, I approach baptism with the understanding that it marks a person's entrance into the household of God. Thus, I use it for those who have been converted as adults and also for the children of believers. Baptism ought to be a joyous and wonderful event!

One of the problems with sacraments is the superstition that sometimes accompanies them. I have had parents want to join the church simply because they knew membership was required before I would baptize their children. They seemed to see baptism as magic, as if it in and of itself would give their children a blessing. I do not believe that baptism saves anyone, but rather that it is a sign and seal of the work of God in saving his folk. I don't believe that infant baptism substitutes for the necessity of a child eventually coming to personal faith in Christ. I do not presumptively declare a child to be born again, because I believe that God's sovereignty trumps our covenant signs (as per Esau in Genesis).

Some disagree with me at this point. I know that God considers children holy (1 Cor. 7:14) and that his declaration therefore makes them eligible for this sign and seal. In this I see it working in the same way as circumcision, which was the mark of the old covenant. Not all physical Israel was spiritual Israel; faith is what the Lord requires of everyone.

In its administration, it is important to explain that baptism is required by God for believers and their families, and it symbolizes the washing by the blood of Christ and the joining of the person to Christ and his work. I really enjoy baptizing the newly converted, and I strongly believe the church needs to celebrate these events, just like the angels in heaven do when a person is saved (Luke 15:10). I love what Carl Ellis has said, "God is always ready to throw another party!"

I don't personally care what mode of baptism is used—sprinkling or immersion. I have baptized by sprinkling. I ask the recipient to kneel. I scoop out as much water as my hands will hold and dump it on. Then I ask the elders to give "the right hand of fellowship" as the new member rises. It is right and proper to sing the doxology or some other praise song after the baptism. I have baptized people in creeks and rivers, and even in a poncho-lined hole in the ground in the desert of Kuwait.

Baptism of new believers is something we should seek to experience frequently, which means we must be about evangelism. Usually baptism should accompany the person's joining the church, which should happen soon after conversion. Pastors should not delay baptism for months until the next class for new members is held. If you have to wait that long for new members to join, something is wrong. Have an individualized membership class if you need to.

We must not ask the baptismal questions in a let's-get-this-over-with-quickly kind of attitude. This is a Gospel opportunity, especially if unsaved friends and family are invited. Preach the Gospel, explain what it does and doesn't mean, and be happy about it!

When babies are baptized, realize that many American Protestant believers find this offensive and confusing since they associate infant baptism with the Catholic Church and have never heard a biblical explanation of it. Its wonderful covenant foundations and covenantal reality need to be taught. Again the Gospel should be articulated while we disabuse the idea that inherited salvation is what is happening. We should spell out that accountability will be required from God for faith as this child comes to understanding. The parents are required to pray for and with their child and to point the child to Christ. The public vow of the congregation to help in the Christian nurture of the child is important. Pastors should occasionally preach a series on the meaning of the sacraments and the vows we take around them.

It is far too easy to be boring when administering a sacrament. Don't read the entire Westminster Confession section about baptism or go through every biblical passage about baptism each time you baptize. But one should not shortchange the people by neglecting an explanation either. If you do your job well in this, the members of your church will grow to have an apologetic they can use concerning baptism, and it will help them remember their own covenantal responsibilities.

It is also too easy to use up a lot of time in the worship service, especially if a pastor-parent or grandparent is baptizing the baby. Decide beforehand which parts of the baptism the guest will perform. Will he read the vows? Sprinkle the water? I suggest having the guest do part but not all of the baptism components so you can make sure the overall worship service stays on track.

The reality of worship production is that as you prepare you must give thought to how its elements will contribute to the length of the service. Sacraments take time, and if you try to include more than one in the same service, it most will likely crowd out the praise time, or preaching time, or lunch time. Consider the time as a whole when planning.

I personally do not like it when pastors baptize people privately, as if the church were not what the person is being baptized into. Baptism is a public event, and unless you are the Ethiopian eunuch on his way back to Ethiopia and will never be seen again, baptism should be a community experience.

I had the joy of being in one congregation where after a person was baptized—child or adult—prayers were offered from members of the congregation for the person. I especially enjoyed hearing the prayers of children, whose theological understanding of what the Christian life and struggle is about was profound. This practice made the covenantal relationship that this person was entering into, not only with the Lord but among the people of God, come alive.

Many Presbyterian congregations today serve a weekly communion, which I heartily support. As I travel the country, I see many different ways congregations observe this sacrament. There seems to be a pastoral movement for a more liturgical experience. Some pastors seem hungry to have a more priestly responsibility in the worship. The pastor has primarily become a liturgist, which I think elevates the clergy as even more than a preacher or elder who has been set apart for teaching.

This is a gross generalization, as there are those of sincere heart who believe that a literary (and it usually is more literary, with readings and responses requiring greater vocabulary and education to appreciate it) and complicated liturgical practice is a more biblical way to worship the true and living God. But I have not heard a lot of biblical justification for adding these things to worship. However, most of the time, in whatever church I find myself on a Sunday morning, I tend to simply worship and not judge the hearts of those who planned it or are leading. Or at least I try not to judge.

When it comes to the administration of the Lord's Supper, I believe it is important to preserve the biblical parameters given for this important part of worship. I have been in too many worship services where there has been no fencing of the table, i.e., mentioning that the elements are for those who take them in faith, after self-examination, and that to take them without faith would be to act in a manner inconsistent with their beliefs and incur judgment. Such parameters to the Lord's Supper are biblical.

If a congregation wishes to celebrate the sacrament every week, pastors should ensure it is still filled with awe, worship, fear, invitation, and joy. This requires communication of its proper meaning each time it is distributed. This is more important than the issue of intinction (dipping the bread into the wine), or who passes the trays, or whether we use wine or juice, or if we should include gluten-free bread.

There is a movement by some to include children in taking of the elements at a very young age or even as babies (this is referred to as paedo-communion). The call for self-examination and words of self-judgment are minimized in such practices. I am not speaking against families bringing children forward for a prayer of blessing. I have nothing against praying for children. Yet sometimes a very young child begs for a piece of bread, and parents simply hand it to him or her. It seems ironic to me that some churches are careful to include the wording from the Book of Church Order about being a member of an evangelical church as part of a warning, but they still do not fence the table in a real way. This implies that a person's membership trumps self-examination.

There is a tender balance in the administration of the Supper between a Gospel-filled understanding of mercy, forgiveness, inclusion in the Body of Christ, and restoration against that of the warnings not to take the meal in an unworthy manner. I suppose some pastors think there can be no unworthy manner if someone is saved, so therefore they give no warnings. I would argue that the warnings were given to the saints at the church at Corinth and they apply now as well.

As I understand it the practice of "fencing the table," this is very different from our Presbyterian forefathers. Their tradition was to take the Lord's Supper only four times a year with congregants appearing the week before to meet with the elders. Members had to have a token of admittance for the actual time of communion to show they had truly given thought to their spiritual condition. I would hate to only experience the Lord's Supper four times a year, but whenever I take it I really want to examine my heart, to hear the Gospel, to remember the Lord's death, and to be thankful I am not only included but that the spiritual presence of Christ to whom I am joined is with me. I am never worthy to take the meal, but Jesus' worthiness is always mine by grace. Hallelujah!

I propose that a tender balance be found between simply reciting words to institute the Lord's Supper and giving a full-fledged second sermon full of warnings that make everyone terrified to actually take it. Such attitudes and teaching are not, I believe, a proper fencing of the table. I need a lot of Romans 8:1 at communion: *"Therefore, there is now no condemnation for those who are in Christ Jesus."*

I encourage pastors to be wise not only in how much time they take in the words of institution but also in what they include or don't include. Be somber, but draw the lines as the Scriptures do. Combine a joyful thankfulness as you call people to rejoice in hope and God's mercy. Call people to reconciliation and communion with each other, and warn them against hypocrisy. It is a balance, and it needs to be carefully done, not simply rushed at the end of the service. Cut your sermon short if you need to so you can set the table properly.

Stop worrying about offending the unsaved and the rebellious. It is a meal of discernment and judgment, and it is not right to attempt to erase the scandal or stumbling block of that. Either you are qualified for the table or you are not, and if you are not then the invitation is to get qualified by coming to Jesus in repentance and faith. The invitation to the lost is not to the table but to Jesus, and once that is taken care of they will be forever invited.

Here are some things I have said in serving the Lord's Table, though not all of them at the same time:

- This is a physical representation of the Gospel that Jesus himself has given to us. This bread represents his body, and the cup his blood. He gave us these tangible things to touch and taste so we would remember him, that he became flesh and dwelt among us. He gave his very real physical self to die for us. If you are a believer, if you have committed your life to Christ and he has saved you, then you are welcome to this table. You are part of the family of God. It is a family meal and only members of the family are welcome to eat it.

- The Scriptures teach (in 1 Cor. 11:28–29) that *"everyone ought to examine themselves before they eat of the bread and drink from the cup. For those who eat and drink without discerning the body of Christ eat and drink judgment on themselves."* This is always a tender part of celebrating communion for many of us. Some of us come to the table with arrogance. We feel we are good enough to take it. No one comes to this table worthy in themselves; we are only worthy by the grace of God and the imputed righteousness of Christ. The only thing we bring to the table, and the cross of which it preaches, is our sin.

- Some of us come with fear, trembling, and a lot of doubt. We don't think we will ever be worthy to take communion, and our unbelief keeps us from the joy of receiving the forgiveness of Christ. One of our beloved hymns says, "Come ye sinners poor and wretched...." Yes, this meal is for real Christians who struggle with their sins, not for the perfect. We are perfected before God in Christ.

- However, take the warning seriously. This Scripture is a bit scary. It says some became sick and some even died because they took it in an unworthy manner (1 Cor. 11:30). Since we are all sinners, how could we be so unworthy that we shouldn't partake? Is there known sin in your life about which you will not repent? Are you living in sin in some way? Is there hate in your heart for some other believer which you will not give up? Please confess your sin to God, ask for the grace of repentance, seek to make things right with your brother or sister if you can, and then come and eat.

- We all need to come to this table with honest humility and real faith, trusting that God is able to forgive us even when we see no way to forgive ourselves. *"This cup is the blood of the new covenant, shed on the behalf of many for the forgiveness of sins"* (Matt. 26:28). Isn't that great? Shed for many, for remission, for forgiveness. Please don't let your doubts keep you from receiving the grace that is yours in Christ. This table is a means of grace for you. Jesus is spiritually present here, and as you take it by faith, he, through his Holy Spirit, can deliver you from your sins and help you live a holy life.

- If you are not yet a disciple and follower of Jesus, we ask that you do not take the Lord's Supper, not yet. We invite you to come to Jesus, to believe in him, and once you do to come and confess your faith to the elders. We will be happy to have you baptized and invite you to this table.
- This table preaches that God is both holy and loving. Sin has been judged and paid for with the blood of Christ so that you and I might be forgiven.

Each pastor should develop his own style while remaining true to the words of Scripture in the administration. He should seek to keep it fresh and thoughtful both for the unsaved, the newly saved, and long-time believers.

CONFESSIONS

In many congregations, sometimes every Sunday, there is a corporate confession of sin. It is traditional to have both a corporate confession of sin and a corporate confession of faith when celebrating communion. I always appreciate churches that provide the corporate confession of sin in their bulletin or program so people can actually read it in advance. It might be good if more worship leaders asked the congregation to take a moment to read any confession of sin prior to saying it out loud.

Some confessions are not traditional. They are written during the week. I don't especially like reading a confession of sin out loud, or any responsive reading, that I have never before had the chance to read if it is not right from Scripture. Generally all the sins we are confessing are genuinely mine, but if I am to sincerely confess my sins then I would, in fact, like to be sincere about it.

Though many Presbyterians identify this as a consistent element of Presbyterian worship, there is nothing scripturally mandated about having a weekly corporate confession of sin. Confession is certainly something we need to be doing, individually and corporately. Yet it is not necessarily an infringement of the Regulative Principle if we leave it out. However, whether the confession is one we do all together or privately in our hearts, we need to be drawn not just to confession but to repentance for our sins.

CHRISTIAN EDUCATION

*If you point these things out to the brothers and sisters, you will
be a good minister of Christ Jesus, nourished on the truths of the
faith and of the good teaching that you have followed.*
1 Timothy 4:6

Most pastors sincerely want spiritual growth for their people; they
want to see Christians become mature in the faith. Ephesians
4:11–16 says it well:

> *So Christ himself gave the apostles, the prophets, the evangelists,
> the pastors and teachers, to equip his people for works of service,
> so that the body of Christ may be built up until we all reach unity
> in the faith and in the knowledge of the Son of God and become
> mature, attaining to the whole measure of the fullness of Christ.
> Then we will no longer be infants, tossed back and forth by the
> waves, and blown here and there by every wind of teaching and by
> the cunning and craftiness of people in their deceitful scheming.
> Instead, speaking the truth in love, we will grow to become in
> every respect the mature body of him who is the head, that is,*

Christ. From him the whole body, joined and held together by every supporting ligament, grows and builds itself up in love, as each part does its work.

One reason you are a pastor is to prepare God's people for works of service. Why should the people serve? *"So that the body of Christ may be built up, until we all reach unity in the faith, in the knowledge of the son of God and become mature, attaining to the whole measure of the fullness of Christ"* (Eph. 4:12–13). Your job as a pastor is not to do all the serving. If that is the case, you are on the road to burnout and bitterness. You also are cheating the very people you are supposed to shepherd, and ultimately depriving them, individually and corporately, of the growth they need.

As I said earlier, many pastors and churches see personal growth primarily as a product of knowledge. However, it is a mistake to think that you are training or teaching your people adequately if all that is happening is that they know more. In Reformed circles, education and learning are highly valued. Unfortunately too many do little or no ministry outside of the home or the local church. We haven't grown until we serve, until we love, until we seek the lost, until we care for others with compassion. Metaphorically speaking, our heads tend to be big while our hands and feet are shriveled up.

To be mature, a believer needs to be putting faith into practice. As we come against the deceitful scheming of people, it is not just their bad ideas or philosophical opposition to our faith that is the problem. Sometimes we are our own worst enemies with our self-centeredness, materialism, racism, and lack of concern for the poor and oppressed. Some in our congregations are lost to unbelief through doubt, immorality, or rebellion, but not usually because their church showed love or stood for justice. If you come from New City Fellowship, it would be hard to take that slander seriously since that is pretty much all we have taught by precept and example.

97

We might have a great apologetic argument to defend the faith, but a very poor one to defend how we live it out. Both are important, and we need to help our church members grow proportionally, in knowledge and practice, by Word and deed. By way of illustration, bodybuilders will make fun of their peers who neglect leg workouts. Our spiritual growth needs to be proportional and multi-dimensional.

Our disciples often look and act just like us. If we do little more than study, our members are likely to do the same. We want our members to know good theology and discern correct doctrine. That includes the parts that call each of us individually and corporately to action.

We must follow the Apostle Paul in preaching the *"whole counsel of God"* (Acts 20:27). In most Reformed circles, that seems to be code for knowing the Five Points of Calvinism or what Romans 9 teaches. Reformed pastors need to remember that our challenge is not to correct all the bad theology in the world. Rather, we need to win lost souls to Jesus. We have evil to withstand, mercy to show, instruction to provide, and justice to cry for. This is the whole counsel we must preach and model.

As a pastor you must think about how you are helping your people learn by precept and example. This means the teaching ministry to the congregation should be comprehensive, extensive, consistent, and practiced. If the pastor thinks he can do all the teaching, and that the only thing the people need are the words from his mouth, he is shortchanging them of the resources available from other believers. The pastor needs to recruit others to help him teach, lead small groups and Bible studies, mentor and disciple the newly converted and young. The more you give ministry away, the faster and larger the church will grow. Growth is not antithetical to Reformed theology, or at least it shouldn't be.

Are parents teaching their children at home? Whatever the struggle in your congregation about public school, preparatory school, Christian school, or home school, parents cannot neglect or leave to others their primary responsibility to teach their children the faith and to live it out before them at home. I am not interested in being legalistic about family devotions, but pastors should encourage and model some method for engaging their member families in learning about and loving Jesus.

Sunday School is a great and wonderful method both for Christian Education and also for evangelism. Pastors should encourage their CE staff to think about tracking what is taught over the years so children gain a wide knowledge of the Word and not simply David and Goliath taught fifty times.

Presbyterians have a great covenantal theology, and thus we focus on our own children and families. This is good, but not at all the complete package for the world in which we live. We will not make a significant impact on our nation for the Gospel until we are willing to raise other people's children too. What I mean is that we cannot neglect the evangelism of children whose parents do not come to church. Our covenantal theology is wonderful, until it becomes an excuse to stay home and fail to bring the lost into the church. Evangelism is an integral part of discipleship, meaning that when we call on people to follow Jesus, we look upon them, right from the moment we meet them, as potentially our future brothers and sisters in Christ, our future elders, deacons, missionaries, and pastors.

As we evangelize children from the community, we need to think of it not as some service project, but as our future. These unsaved (at the moment) children, are people we want to teach, train, and develop as leaders in the church of Jesus Christ. Think of everyone as a potential leader in the church, not simply as a pew sitter or tither, and call each one to further walk with God and serve Jesus.

Unfortunately, we have seen middle-class families react negatively to having community children with their children in a Sunday School class or youth group. There are likely differences in class, knowledge, culture, and behavior. Some families may decide to go to another church so their children feel comfortable and don't have to put up with the "wild" children. This has been one of our hardest challenges in a cross-cultural church that attempts to bring in poor children not accompanied by their parents.

I have seen some church planting models where the church planter is highly enthusiastic about children staying in the worship service. He seeks to have a church where everything is done by family. This sounds very covenantal, but what about the millions of children who live in broken homes? Is there no place for them in our worship, in our churches? I am not asking believers to abandon their own families, but to expand them, to have a heart and compassion for children who are not being raised in the faith. Some of our Reformed congregations simply don't have a theology for unevangelized or unparented children, nor do they yet have the heart or make space for them. This is not how it should be.

TRAINING IN EVANGELISM

But you, keep your head in all situations, endure hardship, do the work of an evangelist, discharge all the duties of your ministry.
2 Timothy 4:5

I have found that unless I plan specific training days or event evangelism it becomes like a cousin I hear about but never see. It is important for pastors not to simply preach an occasional sermon on the subject of witnessing or evangelism, but to model it, to provide opportunities for the people to do it, and to learn ways they can share Christ at school, work, or in their neighborhoods. We have had special Sunday School classes on learning how to share our faith, and we have had special weekend workshops to learn evangelism methods. We have always encouraged our people to share their faith with family, friends, fellow students, and coworkers. Church members at the very least ought to always be inviting people to the church services they attend, and pastors need to remind members to do that.

Here are some questions you can use to assess your members' skills and hearts toward sharing the Gospel:

- Are your members able to share their salvation testimonies with others in less than five minutes?
- Are they able to fold within the story of how they came to faith the actual Gospel story?
- Do they understand the basics of the Gospel story, including: the condition of sinful man, the demonstration of the love of God for the world in sending Jesus, the death of Jesus Christ on the cross for our sins, and his resurrection from the dead?
- Are they faithfully praying for people to come to Jesus?
- Are they praying for people by name?

These are learnable skills and knowledge that the members of any church can practice.

Pastors ought to be asking themselves:

- Has anyone professed faith in Christ through our church this last year?
- Has any adult been baptized after coming to faith in this last year?
- Have I had the opportunity to share Jesus with a nonbeliever lately?
- Am I encouraging my members to be diligent in sharing their faith?
- Are we hearing any salvation testimonies of recent conversions?

If the only reference you have made to and about evangelism in your ministry is about how people are not doing it correctly, there is something wrong, and you are out of balance in your understanding of *"do the work of an evangelist"* (2 Tim. 4:5).

A part of infecting a congregation with the passion for evangelism is to engage them in missions. Presbyterians have a history of problems when it comes to missions and evangelism. Sometimes the practice of foreign missions has become the enemy of local evangelism. Some churches have fairly large missions budgets, and they are usually quite proud of that. They can tell you what percentage of their budget is given to missions and how many missionaries they support. Unfortunately, some of those same churches have no active evangelism going on in their own communities. Some of these churches have even refused to evangelize minorities who live near their church buildings.

We need to understand that not all mission programs, mission boards, or missionaries are the same, or of the same quality or effectiveness. I am afraid some missionaries spend more time writing prayer letters home to raise support than sharing the Gospel with people in their host nations. It is sad when churches raise a lot of money to send teams out on missions trips that don't do any evangelism at all. Some only perform acts of service (which are wonderful and necessary). Others are there only making observations to report back to home base.

Mission trips are great for exposing people to the needs of other communities and giving them hands-on opportunities to share their faith with total strangers. If this is done under the guidance of local pastors and missionaries, it can be very effective. If this is done as part of an effort to plant, build, and grow local churches, then it can be a wonderful experience and a blessing to the people of that area.

However, mission trips can be done in a harmful and wasteful way too, and therefore pastors should provide some quality control and oversight to how the missions program of the congregation, and mission trips in particular, are carried out. Do the missionaries your church supports not only believe what you believe but also practice missions in a way consistent with your own ministry philosophy? If you think missionaries should be sharing the Gospel and working to see people won to Christ, are the missionaries you support doing that?

If you think missionaries should be planting new churches, are they doing that? Are those administrative, medical, translation teams, and logistical support missionaries involved in accomplishing the spearhead program of evangelism and church planting? Just how are they involved in it?

We understand that not everyone is an evangelist or pastor. But we seem to have ended up with too many missionaries who spend a lot of their years building a quality of life for themselves and their families rather than spreading the Gospel, planting churches, or building the Kingdom of God. We need to be asking how are they building a national church, how are they turning over the work to indigenous leadership, and how are they working themselves out of a job?

Missions is not securing a career opportunity for someone to live as an expatriate in a cultural environment they find exciting until they retire. Missions should not be a family business because it is comfortable for children raised on the mission field. Missionary kids can be very useful in missions, but they have to have the Gospel fire inside them as well as cultural adaptability. It is about accomplishing the mission of Christ.

Please don't get me wrong. I think missionaries are some of the coolest people on the planet. The good ones, the best ones, are people of amazing faith, courage, sacrifice, humility, servanthood, and love. They "get" people and seek to understand them. They make friends. They take risks, show hospitality, and champion the poor and oppressed. It is more people like this—the best of our people—that we need to be sending into missions.

Since the end of World War II, there has been a growing missions industry, and the typical American sending congregation is often complicit with that industry. Churches don't ask good questions, they don't evaluate effectiveness, and they don't send their own people to see the people they support in the context of their work. We don't need any more racist missionaries who are colonialist and paternalistic. We don't need any more missionaries who build dependency in national workers and indigenous churches and train them to lean completely on resources from the West.

There are both opportunities and problems in churches sending out mission teams, especially in cross-cultural situations. Many national and indigenous believers love to have mission teams visit because the novelty creates an attraction to the church. They also bring wealth and resources. Many churches in the world are desperately poor, and Western money gives them a boost, as well as the relationships that are created that might create an extended pipeline of help.

On the other hand, mission teams can be poorly trained and led. They can act like tourists, condescending in attitude, and not actively build relationships but rather stay insulated as a group. Money gives a team the power to be demanding, and sometimes those demands can be insulting to the host Christians. The power of money can make missionaries and national workers compromise some of their programs and ministries to make the donors happy. Remember, if you go anywhere on a mission team to help an indigenous church you are there as a guest, a helper, and a servant.

Missionaries should not view mission teams as an interruption or burden. They shouldn't see them them simply as a cash cow, a way to infuse money into their work.

I always wanted more boots on the ground when I hosted mission teams at our church in Chattanooga. We have been able to put them to work in service, train them in evangelism, help them bond as teams in worship, and learn concepts of cross-cultural and mercy ministry. They in turn have inspired many of our own young people, with whom they have worked. I also think mission teams are one of the greatest ways to get lay people excited about the idea of cross-cultural missions and to give them a firsthand view of the needs of the world.

It is naive to think we can end the flow of mission teams and simply send over the money we would have used to take our people there. Money follows people, and fulfilling the task of missions means we need a lot of money to make it happen. We don't apologize for that. However we yearn to see every dollar well spent, well used, and actually creating dynamic and growing national churches in every country and among every ethnic group.

I had the great privilege and benefit of being mentored by a pastor who believed in and practiced evangelism. Pastor Willcox had a drive in him to share the Gospel message with as many people as possible. He wanted to "draw the net" on every presentation of the Gospel so that people would actually decide to ask Jesus to save them. His methods were typically fundamentalist and evangelical. "Every eye closed and every head bowed" was a familiar phrase in our church, and then telling people how to pray the "sinner's prayer" and asking them to raise their hands to indicate they had prayed to receive Christ.

I am sure many of the numbers he counted of those who had "raised their hands" were never really saved. I am also sure that some of them were and came to church, were discipled and baptized, and in turn went out on the streets with us to share the Gospel. My pastor modeled the life of an evangelist. My family also has the great claim of having been led to the Lord by the Rev. Kennedy Smartt, one of the great pastor-evangelists of the Presbyterian Church. Along with these great men, I met and came to know the Rev. William "Bill" Iverson, who also ministered in Newark, New Jersey. I met him when I was ten years old, and for the rest of my life he would be a constant encouragement and model to me in sharing Jesus with everyone.

From middle school on, I was engaged in ministries of the Calvary Gospel Church that were purposefully evangelistic. Every youth group meeting, whether it was the Braves' Club (middle school youth) or the Conqueror's Club (high school youth), ended with a Gospel presentation. I am pretty sure I heard every illustration my pastor had at least ten times—and they were not boring—because I was caught up in praying for God to bless the message and win my fellow teens to Christ.

I was called on many times in my youth to give a salvation testimony. I was trained to speak in open-air meetings and present a short Gospel story, usually with a paint brush in my hand, so I could visually illustrate what I was talking about. By the time I was in high school, I was being picked up after school on just about every Thursday to help my pastor conduct an open-air children's meeting. In the summer, I attended week-long Open Air Campaigner seminars to learn how to do evangelism effectively. They had no intention of standing on corners simply to shout at people; they intended to draw a crowd and hold the people's attention, and it worked!

Along with the open-air work, I joined a group called Hi-B-A, or High School Born-Again-ers (High School Evangelism Fellowship). Every Friday I would either walk to the club or get picked up. At Hi-B-A we (Joan was also in this group) would memorize Scripture that we could use to share Jesus with our peers, and we would learn techniques of how to open an evangelistic conversation. One of my great joys is to know a certain lady who is now a member in my home church who came to Christ simply because I carried my Bible to school and covered it in a bright orange book cover. "What is that?" she asked. Soon she came to Conqueror's Club, and then saved, and now she is serving Jesus.

Paul's words in 2 Timothy 4:5, *"Do the work of an evangelist,"* are essential to being a faithful pastor. My home pastor might have been out of balance in his pursuit of evangelism or his pursuit of young people. I am sure members wanted more out of him in counseling, visitation, or greater training in various areas. But I will forever be in awe of him and his wife for the time they gave to hundreds of children, young people, and adults in all kind of situations so as to share Jesus and call people to faith. They spent hours and hours picking up urban kids for youth group and then taking them home. I have never matched him or lived up to his efforts, but part of the compulsion for me to preach the Gospel is because of the impact he had on my life.

He taught me to always think about including the Gospel message in my sermons, and I believe every pastor needs to remember that. He made me unafraid to give a Gospel invitation, but I have also learned to try to do it honestly and without manipulation. He taught me to look for Gospel opportunities and take them, and he taught me boldness and courage.

I learned many methods over the years, from the Four Spiritual Laws of Campus Crusade, to the two diagnostic questions of Evangelism Explosion from Coral Ridge. I am Reformed in my theological convictions, so I see some of the problems of an Arminian approach to evangelizing. It is God who saves people and not me. It is the Holy Spirit who opens the spiritual eyes and hearts of people and not my methods. It is the Holy Spirit who uses his Word to bring people to faith and not my arguments. I am a presuppositionalist that tries to persuade men. Believing in the sovereignty of God, I find it an amazing coincidence that people don't get saved if Christians fail to share Jesus with their relatives, friends, neighbors, and strangers. As the Apostle Paul said, *"Knowing the fear of God I persuade men"* (2 Cor. 5:11).

How could any of us read the Scriptures and fail to see that the apostles and early believers zealously and passionately shared their faith with those who were lost? We are commanded to go, to make disciples of all the nations, to teach them, and to baptize them. We see an example of how the early church spread the Gospel, and we in turn are told to preach and share it. Yet it seems we spend a lot of our time developing theological arguments as to why someone's methods aren't biblical rather than going out ourselves to proclaim Christ. I just have to say this—almost any method I use (and I certainly try to be faithful to the truth of Scripture) is more biblical than not using any method at all.

What method do you teach your people to use? How do you model evangelism for your people? How have you infected your church with a personality of evangelism? At our church, I tried to use open-air children's meetings to foster a programmatic approach, where every summer we have gone to people in inner city neighborhoods sharing Jesus. I used this method to teach the basics of a

Gospel presentation. There is nothing slick about it, nothing very intellectual. It is a method where we actually show up in a neighborhood, often not knowing anyone who lives there, and begin to preach Christ. We actually tell them exactly what we are going to do, and they still bring their children to hear the Bible stories.

One of our methods has been to hold a children's meeting at the same place for three nights, take kids on a picnic later that week, and then invite them to Urban Camp at the end of the summer. We then recruit them to our soccer league, or our tutoring program, or our youth groups. Over the years we have seen many young people profess faith, come into the church, and come with their families.

It is interesting to me how many pastors seem to despise evangelizing children. It is almost as if they don't believe children can be converted, nor do they seem to want to take the effort to use children's evangelism to reach the parents. It seems many pastors want a method by which adults, and usually a socially acceptable kind of adult, will readily accept Jesus, eventually be baptized, and join the church.

There could be several reasons for this kind of evangelistic snobbery or abdication. Evangelizing children might mean kids without parents will want to come to church, and they may be hard to control. Pastors may be lazy when it comes to organizing a sufficient structure of moving from evangelizing to gathering and discipling. Pastors could feel insufficient in communicating with kids. They might feel their theological training is being wasted in such efforts. Children just don't seem to need to know all the pastor knows yet. It is no wonder that one generation after another in our country is seeing fewer and fewer children come to Christ, at the very ages when most people historically are most open to the faith.

SUGGESTIONS

1. More of Christ and less of you is what people need to hear in your sermons. Seek to promote faith. You teach your people knowledge, but that is not your goal. You want your people to do good works, but that is not your goal. You want your people to be holy, but that is not your goal. The way we bring glory to God through preaching is to call people to believe, trust, and have faith in Jesus! Everything else happens and comes together because of the power and victory that comes through God's people believing his Word (Gal. 5:6). Our obedience comes through faith.

Never waste a sermon, at least not by a casual attitude that a particular sermon doesn't matter. People are saved and their lives are changed by preaching, so you should approach it as a matter of life and death. The Reformed pastor Richard Baxter said, "I preach as a dying man to dying men."[1]

2. Don't wait for your own moral perfection before you preach. The only perfect man who preached was Jesus. Holiness comes through the covering of the righteousness of Christ, which we have by grace through faith and in our union with him. It is not simply that we had a good week of not consciously breaking the command-

ments. Grace also gives us the faith to pursue that righteousness. It is evidenced by an honest, broken, and repentant heart.

Aim for the human heart, which is a combination of our thinking, feeling, and volition. The preacher must address all three. Preaching is cognitive, but it is also emotional. It is science in terms of knowing the text, proper exegesis, and interpretation, but it is also art in its delivery and call for a response on the part of the listener.

3. Know the cultural context well, since all preaching occurs in a cultural context. Consider how your content, style, and delivery will be received. Learn from the technique of Jesus. The greatest preacher who ever preached told stories. He used them to help people drop their defenses so he could stab them in their moral hearts.

4. Pray while you preach. If while preaching you feel you are failing, then pray in your heart for God to uphold you. If you feel you are doing well, pray that you will not preach in your own strength. Be wary of any sort of hubris in regards to your preaching. It is corrosive to your soul. Remember you are engaged in spiritual warfare as you preach.

Develop a method that allows you to preach whole books. Stop waiting for blinding inspiration about what text you should preach next Sunday. All Scripture is worth preaching.

5. Beware of ruts and hobby horses. Avoid anything that seems to regularly appear in your preaching that might become competition with the Gospel of grace and the glory of God. If you are against racism, sex before marriage, divorce, communism, the Democratic or Republican parties, etc., beware that you don't keep wiggling your agenda into every text.

6. Preach Christ and grace from the Old Testament. If you preach

the Old Testament without seeing Jesus or grace in it, then you don't yet understand it. We are not seeking typology in every Old Testament text, but the question remains: What place does this text occupy in redemptive history?

7. Don't wander from your text or simply read a text at the beginning and then fail to preach it. Not to preach the text you read is like telling people your ideas are more important than the Bible.

8. Application is essential. Simply reading the text and explaining it is not preaching. How do you live out the Scripture? My homiletics professor, Dr. Rayburn, used to stress that we should ask ourselves: What does God want me to do? We need to ask those in our flock the same, along with much hope in grace from God to help us do it.

Apologize publicly. If you make a mistake in preaching (you misinterpreted a text, or were flippant, angry, or insulting) apologize publicly the next time you are before your people.

Never belittle, ridicule, or embarrass your wife and children in illustrations for your sermon. The congregation will take their side and miss the spiritual point you were trying to make. Once your kids reach middle school, avoid mentioning them like the plague.

9. Pay attention to your wife's reactions and watch her face. She is probably the most loyal critic you have. Listen to her suggestions.

10. Don't indulge in self-criticism or criticism from others too quickly after a sermon. Criticism of your sermon is a good thing if you seek it from those who want to help you, but give yourself some time after you preach. Let your ego heal from its vulnerability. Likewise, avoid arguments or being defensive right after you preach, as sometimes people come up immediately to correct or rebuke you. Ask them to make an appointment.

11. Be honest; admit it is not original to you if it isn't. Attribute, cite, and give credit where you should. Borrow ideas ruthlessly; just admit it and protect your integrity. Never plagiarize.

12. Use preaching devices for impact, but avoid letting them become a distraction. Use alliteration to help people remember the points, or use one repeated phrase as a hook on which to hang the main idea of the sermon. Using a riff to rattle off a list of powerful ideas or applications (e.g., starting each item in the list with the same phrase) can be very effective, especially if you have rhythm. Learn to preach with rhythm.

13. Learn when to stop talking. Discern the ability of your people to absorb what you are saying. They can't take in all that you have learned from your study in one sermon. John Perkins once told me, as he was told by a host pastor where he spoke, "Preach as long as you like, but when you are done preaching, stop talking!"

14. Learn how to use invitations, physical responses, and calls to the front with purpose, clarity, and without manipulation. Don't promise salvation for walking forward, but you can invite people to come up and pray with elders.
Be aware of the emotions you project. Being angry in your preaching is not usually helpful. Be mindful of your demeanor and what emotions you are communicating.
When you preach have a sense of God's presence and preach in the fear of him.

15. When you preach believe that the Word of God is living and powerful and that God's Word will accomplish that which he intends. Believe that the Gospel is the power of God to save and to change people. Preach like you mean it!

---

1. Adapted from Richard Baxter, "Love Breathing Thanks and Praise" in *The Poetical Fragments of Richard Baxter*, 4th ed. (London: W. Pickering, 1821), 35.

PART FIVE

SHEPHERDING

CARING FOR THE PEOPLE OF GOD

Be shepherds of God's flock that is under your care.
1 Peter 5:2

The work of the ministry is holy. Ministry is set apart by God to accomplish his will. We know that all believers are priests, what we call "the priesthood of believers" (1 Pet. 2:5). We don't all have the same gifts, nor do we all have the same calling. To be set apart for the teaching ministry of the church means you follow in the calling of the priests of the Old Testament (in regard to their teaching and guidance) and the elders of the New Testament. We don't offer sacrifices for the atonement of sin. Jesus Christ is our sacrifice, and our Great High Priest. He offered himself for our sins.

Though this book is about the reality of our insufficiency, it is also a book on pastoral competence. There must be some standard or measure of knowledge and skill required to do the job of pastoring if you wish to do it well. That standard of competence, aside from your own conscience before the Scriptures and the Lord, is often up to the expectations of the flock you pastor.

If your church becomes exasperated with your performance as

a pastor, it will eventually seek a change. Hopefully it will first appeal to you for a higher standard of performance. You might not realize how upset they are until they call for your replacement or decide they want to seek another church in which to worship. No matter how we might complain about the consumerism of church members, God's people do expect, and need, competence from their pastors.

This is one of the challenges of training pastors for ministry. Seminaries are usually focused on the necessity of knowledge. They provide an academic preparation for ministry but not always a practical one. They don't usually measure or train students in skills. Homiletics, or preaching, might be the one major practical skill they teach.

LEADERSHIP

Obey your leaders and submit to their authority.
They keep watch over you as men who must give an
account. Obey them so that their work will be a joy, not a
burden, for that would be of no advantage to you.
Hebrews 13:17

In a Barna Research Group poll of pastors, 70 percent responded that they did not want to lead. I was sorry to read this statistic but not actually surprised. If it is true that many men go into the ministry because they are people pleasers, it stands to reason that leadership would be something they would want to avoid. Because when you lead, you have opposition. It is the nature of the beast.

Many of us went into the ministry because of a sincere love for God and his Word. It is, most of the time, a joy to read the Bible, learn more about God, and learn to love God more and more. It is a pleasure to spend time studying theology, church history, and to think about spiritual things. If the only things we had to do were spend time in our study, get up and preach, and then be loved (and paid) by the people for it, that would be a good life.

However, most churches hire pastors to be more than simply a scholar. They want someone to shepherd them personally and as a group. They want someone who will counsel, help them through hard times, and settle conflicts. They want someone to help them as an organization, to give a sense of vision and direction to the congregation.

As soon as a leader says "this" and not "that," then there will be those who defend the "that" and take issue with the leader. If the pastor hates conflict and wants very badly to be liked, he may test the wind to see which way it is blowing before saying anything. Even worse, once he hears any opposition, he may quickly change his mind, confusing everyone as to where he stands on an issue. Or out of pride and fear, he may not be able to listen and compromise with strength, so he becomes dictatorial. Being a tyrant sometimes counterfeits as leadership, but it is not good leadership.

One test of leadership is whether the leader and his followers know where they are going. The leader's influence through his character, encouragement, and articulation of a compelling vision gives people confidence to follow him. Unfortunately some leaders choose to rely on the strength of an established organization by which they were hired and bring no fresh challenge to their people. Many of us have watched once great and active churches plateau in their impact and then decline because of new leaders who have no vision.

Pastors who refuse to lead are like captains on a ship who refuse to set a course. They enjoy the sailing but never seem to get anywhere except by accident. Eventually these churches sense a great need for renewal and revival. Churches would do well to not call pastors who are merely managers of stability or a maintainer of a legacy.

Unfortunately many pastors simply don't know how to combine the mandates of Scripture, the cultural context, and the historical legacy of congregation and community with the needs of the surrounding population and society. They neither feel nor communicate a sense of need, urgency, and opportunity. They seem content to have a job that allows them to study, preach, and have status as the church declines in membership and Gospel impact. We cry, Lord have mercy!

I think it fair to use myself as an example, for better or worse, in this area of leadership. I consider leadership to be one of the gifts the Lord gave me, and then he gave me the formal position of leadership by making me a pastor. The Army tried to give me a lot of teaching and training about leadership. I became a collector of military history and immersed myself in the biographies and stories of military and political leaders. Many of those stories are cautionary tales and not always inspirational. I wish I had been a better leader and more effective. I have been abundantly blessed by the fact that people chose to follow me, and I can only hope that they were blessed in the following. Leadership in the church is a spiritual gift and also a learned skill.

One of the first things a leader has to do is cast vision. I assume that matters of character, integrity, knowledge, and wisdom are a foundation that must be already present in a pastor. My experience in my youth was mostly about "Do!" I followed (and learned a lot from) a leader who had an agenda. He knew what he wanted to get accomplished, and he recruited, trained, motivated, and deployed others to get things done. As I pursued my education, took on part-time ministry jobs, and was given various leadership roles, it became important for me to figure out the "why" of things. What are we trying to accomplish and why? With that I then had to help myself and others figure out the "how" of getting things done. Sometimes I was told by those who gathered around me, "Just tell us what to do!" One of my dominant personality traits is to be a director. At first blush that may appear to be great for a leader, but bossing people around is not in and of itself leadership.

I was given a lot of ministry responsibility early in my life, and people trusted me. I confess that some of that trust was probably misplaced, and I am sure that what people thought was competence and confidence was sometimes bravado and ego, along with presumptuousness. If I had been wiser, I would have had more fear, but I think I just naively expected for things to get better. I wish I had been more self-aware of my own sinfulness and weakness.

I expected progress because I believed God was big. I expected him to do big things, even though I never felt my faith was all that strong. I had the idea that problems in the community were actually opportunities for the power of God and the ministry of his people.

I had a passion to tell people about Jesus. I had a desire to gather young people together and teach them the Bible. I wanted to take the Gospel to the poorest neighborhoods in the city. I had a passion to bring African Americans who were unchurched into the church and for people from various ethnic groups to love each other and worship together. I did not start with a detailed scheme about how this was going to be done, but I knew the general direction and that is where I pointed anybody who came around me. I had an increasing awareness of prevalent injustice and the need to change it.

My sense of what the vision should be for the specific church God called me to pastor grew and developed. The necessity for the growth of that vision was that it was not always clear what the racial dynamic or culture might demand. I was a young White man married to a young African American woman, working in an African American neighborhood, accompanied by well-meaning middle-class White people. These were mostly faculty, staff, and students from a Christian college. There were then, and still are today, various opinions about the validity of the whole enterprise.

I had a ton of questions. Were we right to even want to start this kind of church? Should I be the one to try to start the church and then later see if we could call an African American pastor to take over? How long should I stay? Would Black people come to the church in any significant numbers? If I stayed on as pastor, would it turn into a paternalistic kind of ministry that would always have

White leadership? Would I be respected by Black leaders? Would I have their cooperation and help? How would I know when to leave if that was what God wanted?

Seeing that we have consistently attracted White people, it may sound strange (to those who don't know my background) that I never expected White middle-class folks to follow me. I honestly felt foreign to that culture.

I learned what it means to be a target when in leadership, especially when others don't think you should be in that role. One of the constants in human life and society are sinful attitudes arising from envy, jealousy, and resentment. These become corrosive behaviors in people and can infect an institution.

Often those holding such feelings are not open and honest about them. They might not be able to discern why they feel the way they do, or they may feel guilty about having such feelings but are unable to resolve them. This emotional confusion often leads to a passive-aggressive opposition that many pastors experience. This kind of negative-competitive ambition within individuals has been present in many military and political institutions and has caused a great deal of harm. I think of the passage from Proverbs 26, beginning at verse 23:

> *Like a coating of glaze over earthenware are fervent lips with an evil heart. A malicious man disguises himself with his lips, but in his heart he harbors deceit. Though his speech is charming, do not believe him for seven abominations fill his heart. His malice may be concealed by deception, but his wickedness will be exposed in the assembly. If a man digs a pit, he will fall into it; if a man rolls a stone, it will roll back on him. A lying tongue hates those it hurts, and a flattering mouth works ruin.*

This corresponds to James 3:14–16:

> *But if you harbor bitter envy and selfish ambition in your hearts,*

do not boast about it or deny the truth. Such "wisdom" does not come down from heaven but is earthly, unspiritual, of the devil. For there you have envy and selfish ambition, there you find disorder and every evil practice.

I have been on the receiving end of this kind of behavior, and at first it is confusing because you don't know why you are being attacked and sometimes don't even know by whom. My actual sins are usually worse than the lies that have been told about me, but I can say, "I been lied about, sure as you're born."

In my leadership in a cross-cultural situation, I have realized that some African American brothers did not want to serve with me or under me. Sometimes leadership competition (especially in young men) is an issue as a new organization or congregation is trying to figure out who is going to be the leader, and different men want the top position or feel they deserve it. When you add race to that, competition matters can become confusing. Someone might feel he did or did not get a position because of race. Though racism is a relevant issue generally, it is not always applicable particularly. In other words, there may be other factors determining who gets hired or not.

In the world of cross-cultural church planting, there are lots of racial and missional issues when it comes to the ethnic make-up of churches and their leadership. When we planted New City Fellowship in Chattanooga, the prevailing ideas about church growth were coming from Fuller Seminary's School of Church Growth and the writings of Dr. Donald McGavran and C. Peter Wagner. They were teaching the idea of the Homogeneous Unit Principle, which generally states that people want to be with people who are like them, including in church.[1]

Critics of our small and young church thought our only hope to be successful would be to follow that principle, or else we would just produce a paternalistic congregation with some token representation of Black folks. In short, they did not believe multiethnic or cross-cultural churches could be successful.

Not only was there a philosophical confusion and critique about the way to do what we were doing, but it affected me personally. I felt judged by some of my peers and wondered if I could ever be validated as being genuine, or being needed, in and for this work. Some held the idea that only Black men should pastor Black people and that White people would never accept a Black pastor. There appeared to be historical evidence and cultural, social reasons for these opinions.

As far as I know my heart, I don't think I held onto New City with a tight grip. I didn't own it. Even though I believe God used my entrepreneurial personality, my assertive determination to preach the Gospel and gather people into a church, I knew that I didn't create it by myself. Even if I helped to start the church, it wasn't mine to control. I was responsible to shepherd it as long as God told me to do it and not one minute longer.

I was subject to my elders, listened to them, and sometimes called them out of their negative, sinful, and divisive behavior. There were attacks from both outside and within the church, but as time went on I saw many of the myths about a cross-cultural church dispelled. Black and White folks wanted to worship together. Black folks and White folks both wanted me to preach and accepted my pastoring of them. Both Black men and White men could be jealous of me and oppose my leadership and choose to walk away when we needed them. I could and did hand the reigns of leadership over to other men, especially African American men, and I saw the church honor, respect, and follow them. I was held in esteem, given respect, included, loved, listened to, and even followed by some great African American men and women. It continues to humble me, and I am tremendously honored and grateful for their support.

The reality of race and racism makes people vulnerable to what we call playing the "race card." Sometimes there is a glass ceiling in an organization or church. Sometimes there is prejudice in deciding whether or not a Black man will be the one given the mantle of leadership or be denied it. Sometimes, however, race is not the basis for giving or denying the mantle of leadership. I remember hearing a young African American seminary graduate on my staff say out loud, "Why you?" It was a question about me and the validity of my leadership role.

Actually it is a great question and made me think a lot about grace. I only stayed in this calling, endured, survived, and prospered by grace. It was almost as if he were asking why he wasn't allowed to just take over, as if to dismiss the sacrifice that was necessary to start the work and all that I had done for the previous thirty years. Every once in a while, I had the suspicion that people thought I had taken this job away from someone else instead of creating it from scratch.

Of course, anyone who wants to have a ministry like New City is always welcome to go start another one. Especially today as compared to when we started, there are networks and organizations with money that can give a young ambitious pastor all kinds of resources to start a church. Sometimes that money is wasted on an individual who has more ambition than he has skill or godliness. But sometimes the leverage of resources gives a gifted man a fast start. The test of time shows whether he has the wisdom, spirituality, and faith to back up his charisma so that he plants, builds, and leads a healthy congregation.

As I look back at my lack of qualifications to be a successful pastor, and here I speak not of intelligence or education or passing the ordination tests (I did pass!), I can say with Paul that:

> But he said to me, "My grace is sufficient for you, for my power is made perfect in weakness." Therefore I will boast all the more gladly about my weaknesses, so that Christ's power may rest on me. That is why, for Christ's sake, I delight in weaknesses, in insults, in hardships, in persecutions, in

difficulties. For when I am weak, then I am strong. 2 Cor. 12:9–10

I think the fact that I was (and still am!) White was just one aspect of my weakness, so I guess I will have to boast of it. Being raised in poverty without a dad, with no impulse control, with loneliness, with a lot of psychological needs—all of those are my weaknesses—means I will boast about them because any success came from God's grace, mercy, and the power of Christ.

There were others who wondered why I had the position I had. At first this was because I was fairly young to be a pastor and church planter. Others questioned because I was a White man serving in a predominantly African American community. I admit there were others who doubted my fitness because I was inept in some areas, and they simply didn't think much of my abilities.

Leadership may be a formally appointed or elected position. Some people will respect the leader simply because that leader holds the designated position. Others will hold back respect until they feel the leader earns it. However you have it, in a formal or informal way, it is always more powerful when the leader earns respect.

That earning is subjective in a follower and comes from all manner of things. The follower may appreciate the experience, education, giftedness, character, work ethic, sacrifice, or wisdom of the leader. None of those things automatically make a person accepted as a leader, but they may make it easier for people to follow him.

The Bible says, *"Lay hands suddenly on no man..."* (1 Tim. 5:22). Leaders need to be tested in some way to see whether they have staying power and whether they can handle increased authority without ruining their character. If elevation to leadership happens too quickly, especially without some kind of protection through accountability, it can ruin both individuals and the organization that needs them to function with integrity.

Circumstances might suddenly force leadership on an individual. Sometimes this works out better than anyone could hope or expect, and at other times it doesn't. Sometimes ambition makes an individual strive for a position of power, or he may see it as a step toward economic security and a job. Worse, some simply desire it to keep someone else from getting it. Congregations and organizations need to be careful that in their quest to find leaders, especially in the legitimate desire to see minority leadership raised up, that they don't grab the first man they see and anoint him. It is terrible to set someone up for failure if and when he is not qualified for certain ministry positions.

Race is no guarantor for competence or holiness. There are some capable White men who are cross-culturally skilled and called, but they are few in my experience. I would say the same about Black men, and being Black or a minority does not mean one automatically has cross-cultural ministry skills. One might be experienced as a minority in living cross-culturally, as most have to be in a White-dominated society, but that doesn't always equate to ministry skills or loving in a multiethnic community. Cross-cultural ministry skills can be learned and sharpened, and those should be pursued intentionally, tested, and validated, but not assumed.

My responsibility was to cast an ideological vision (concepts of culture, context, the path to growth, and an idea of what we were trying to be) and then to police that vision on behalf of our congregation. I had to develop what our congregation was to be about and how that would be reflected in our worship, ministries, staff, and mission. Then, as someone steering the ship toward a certain destination, I had to make sure that all the choices we made culturally and ethnically reflected a commitment to that vision. We had to intentionally keep striving toward the goal. At the very least, I had to be ready to give an apologetic for the kind of music that we sang, the people that we hired, and how we spent our money.

Sometimes subtraction is the fastest way to growth. Sometimes those who oppose the direction of the ministry need to leave so that everybody can start rowing in the same direction. What I mean is that inevitably there will be people who come into conflict with the leadership. This might be due to personality, jealousy, envy, or pure orneriness. Sometimes the conflict is because someone honestly doesn't agree with the stated vision or the strategy to get there. Our elders had a commitment to be a cross-cultural church, to be evangelistic, and a congregation that tried to minister mercy to the poor and stand up for justice.

The most dangerous prayer a pastor can pray, or so I have been told is, "Lord, change them or move them." It is dangerous because it seems you have just asked the Lord to do whatever he wants to those who oppose you (even death) if he needs to get them out of the way. I was conscious of this possibility on the rare times I prayed that prayer about an individual, knowing that God would do anything he thought necessary to keep building his church, no matter the opposition. I feared God and had the conviction that this applied to me as well if I was an obstacle.

I didn't always get it right, but it was my honor to have one day been accused of being "tenaciously cross-cultural." Yes, that is what I wanted and want to be! There were White people who thought I should be more open to leaving that vision behind, or that it would just come about naturally and that I was wrong to be so insistent on it. There were Black people who thought a church couldn't be cross-cultural until a Black man led it, and I stepped aside. It was interesting to me that when I did in fact step down and a Black man took over as senior pastor that there were Black pastors who seemed to take it that this step was finally the fulfillment of being truly cross-cultural. The attitude I picked up was that now New City had finally arrived.

We never arrive fully (until heaven), as being cross-cultural is always a goal, a missional journey. In a sense, we had arrived at being cross-cultural when we set it as our intention to be so, though it would take years before the congregation's ethnic mix actually represented our dream. We have achieved an institution that has stood as a cross-cultural ministry for more than fifty years, so I can joyfully say "to God be the glory!" Yet it is always a struggle, always in a dynamic process and flow. This vision always has to be policed; the course always has to be corrected, sometimes very slightly and sometimes aggressively. Having a united group of leaders made this much easier for me, and I am sure a unified and supportive leadership makes it easier for any pastor.

One aspect of leadership is being able to cast vision for specific aspects of the ministry of the church. Does the pastor have a vision for how his elders or leadership group should function and what they are supposed to achieve? If a pastor has no concept of how to build a leadership team or what the leadership should cohesively and in a unified way accomplish, he will create a leadership vacuum and negative and reactionary ideas may fill that space.

Does the pastor have a vision for mercy ministry and how the deacons or mercy team should function and for what they should be trying to accomplish? Here is the strange thing: We all expect the pastor to train officers, but they are often clueless in how to do it and don't have a theology of mercy. The pastor doesn't know it should be done in a way that really helps the poor and suffering. How could it mobilize and bless the church at the same time?

Leaders shouldn't decide that, since they are ignorant, they then can neglect those areas of ministry needed in and for their congregations. They need to get training. They need not only to recruit gifted practitioners but to build systems that accomplish the vision which he has cast, and to keep producing (recruiting, training, and deploying) such people who can take up responsibility when positions need to be refilled, which is inevitable in church life.

---

1. Donald McGavran, *Understanding Church Growth*, 3rd ed., rev. and ed. C. Peter Wagner (Grand Rapids, MI: Eerdmans, 1990); C. Peter Wagner, *Our Kind of People: The Ethical Dimensions of Church Growth in America* (Atlanta, GA: John Knox, 1979).

ADMINISTRATION

God has appointed... those with gifts of administration.
1 Corinthians 12:28

The gift of administration is not given to everyone and does not automatically descend from heaven on everyone who is ordained as a pastor. The gifts of leadership and administration are two distinct gifts. One can be a great administrator and a terrible leader, or a great leader and terrible administrator. Know your gifts and your strengths and play to them. Find someone else to help you with the gifts you don't have. In other words, staff your weakness!

People used to make fun of me and my congregation because of my weakness in administration and organization. We made fun of ourselves by saying, "If you don't like the organized church then come to New City." Organization is an aspect of administration. Thankfully we had a very organized elder who helped us over and through some of our rough spots. I am grateful to the late Rudy Schmidt for all that he did in managing our money and records. He made sure things got done, and he kept me out of most of the trouble I kept getting into.

How in the world James Ward (our music and worship director) and Rudy were willing to work with me and allow me to be their pastor is really beyond me. Both of these men knew how to administrate and organize, and there have been times when I completely frustrated them. Making appointments and forgetting them was one of my biggest faults. One of my biggest deficiencies was not hiring an executive pastor to run the staff and church calendar but for many years we didn't have the money to do that. I am grateful to the secretaries who tried hard to keep me pointed in the right direction.

Since stepping down as a senior pastor, after overseeing a growing staff of full-time, part-time, and volunteer workers, I have been asked, "What were some of your biggest mistakes?" There were many. As far as administration goes though, it was hiring the wrong people and then not firing them fast enough once I realized they were not a good fit.

The ability to hire qualified and gifted people, supervising, holding them accountable to clear standards, and then letting folks go or "firing" them is hard in every organization. In a church it is even more problematic. The employees are not just staff but usually members of the church. The organization is not just a business but also a church, and people expect it to be more compassionate and understanding in how it deals with those who work there. I believe in compensating people fairly, as I want to be. I believe in giving people benefits, as I want them too. I believe in keeping workers safe and healthy, and in giving them days off and vacation. However, my beliefs did not always match up well with the church budget.

I learned several hard lessons in hiring folks. One lesson, and this was decidedly taught to me by Rudy, was to beware of those who want to come on staff and say they will raise their own support. As soon as they are on staff, it always seems like their support dries up and then they appeal to the conscience of the church to make up the difference. These are difficult calls, but it is wise to think ahead to the worst-case scenario. We should look a gift horse in the mouth. If someone is on staff without getting much if any income from the congregation, he can become bitter, and bitterness always seems to spread.

Another lesson I learned was to beware of hiring people to help them financially and not necessarily because they are the best fit for the job. There are always jobs that need filling in an active church, but once someone has a position, it becomes much more difficult if you have to let him or her go. Every staff member represents the church, so incompetence affects the church's reputation.

I hope I have learned to listen to others, which at times I failed to do. I have announced my desire to hire for a certain position, and staff or church members warned me that the person I was considering might not be a good fit. In almost every situation I was proved wrong, and those who gave advice were proved correct.

Establishing a personnel committee to vet applicants can help, and leaders should not dismiss their recommendations and just hire who they want. Once the pastor or supervisor realizes the person hired is not performing well, and that attempts at coaching, training, reprimanding, or correcting have all failed, then action to dismiss should be taken swiftly. The pressure to delay due to personal relationships, church politics, or sympathy for the person's family situation ends up harming the church. All of us on staff are only there as servants of the congregation, and if the church is not being served well, then things must change. This is not to say that the church shouldn't provide a good or compassionate severance package.

Staff members in a congregation are an extension of each pastor's ministry. If someone is hurting the ministry because of lack of productive work, or because of negative influence on other staff or church members, or because of sinful behavior, and the pastor takes no action to change the situation, then the resulting damage is the fault of the pastor.

Pastor Sandy Wilson (when he was the pastor of Lookout

Mountain Presbyterian Church) once told me that he decided early on as a senior pastor (who had to supervise staff) that he would fire any staff member who was attacking other staff or members behind their backs. He would let new staff members know this policy at the beginning of their employment. I tried to adopt his policy, and I believe he was correct in seeking to protect the unity and peace of the staff, and thus the church.

Sometimes letting people go is simply a financial reality. Budgets aren't always met. Sometimes they shrink, and church financial committees or church treasurers try to find ways for the church to pay its bills. I always hated this reality because sometimes it meant people that I had hired, loved, and needed had to be asked to step down. My only joy in this was to see those same people remain in the church and continue to worship with us. This spoke more of their loyalty to God and love for the church than in our treatment of them. However, I am very grateful for the love and care we tried to shower on those who worked for us. At New City our staff has usually displayed a strong work ethic, so it has not always been an easy place to work. It was often exciting but not always easy.

Sometimes people that are let go become bitter. They take no ownership of their own failures. Sometimes this is simply their attempt to rewrite their employment history with the church to justify themselves. It is important for every pastor or personnel supervisor in a church to document not only their decisions but also the process that led to them. It is important to make sure the collective leadership is kept informed and allowed to speak into healing relationships.

Another thing to mention under administration is something I learned from my pastor, Grover Willcox. He was careful to tell me to keep my hands off the church checkbook. He advised me never to take the responsibility of having the "say so" over spending church funds, but only to do this under the authority of the church officers. This was great advice, and it spared me (and them) from any of my habits of negligence or mismanagement hurting the congregation. This is not to say that my voice as a leader didn't count in the session or in the congregation in terms of where we should spend our money. But even as I led, others kept track of the money.

CONFLICT

*Make every effort to keep the unity of the
Spirit through the bond of peace.*
Ephesians 4:3

When our congregation acquired a new building, some of the folks from the former congregation that met there decided to remain with us. One lady in particular came and told me in no uncertain terms that she was in charge of the kitchen. She told me she would happily recruit other church women to help pull off the various church suppers and socials that we might have in the future. At first I thought this was great since she knew the facility and seemed eager to merge into our congregation.

I had no idea how much trouble her staking out territory would cause. She did develop a group of women who helped in the various uses of the kitchen. At the same time, we had a formal women's group in our congregation. I always tried to be supportive of them. The women's group had an annual election and chose particular individuals to be in charge of particular events, one of which was the Easter breakfast. This group was seeking to be cross-cultural, dividing up responsibilities so that both Black and White women were included.

The woman who claimed authority of the kitchen had for the most part only recruited White women. They were all good women. However, when this lady heard that the women's group had chosen someone other than her to lead an event, she was livid. She had not attended their meeting and had given no voice to her concerns. Instead she called me and told me I needed to straighten the women's group out and let them know she would handle things. In coming years, we would go on to have other individuals argue over the kitchen. I guess it is inevitable as people try to help, and others try to take control, and still others ignore those who also wish to help.

In short order, I found myself caught in the middle of two groups of women about the use and authority of the kitchen. I told this woman who had demanded sole authority that I could not and would not overrule an established women's group in the church. I did encourage her to try and work things out with them. Instead she and some of the ladies she had organized (with their families) left the church.

One of the skills needed by pastors in the exercise of their leadership is dealing with conflict. I hope some of these ideas help you when you go through conflict. If you are a pastor, you surely will.

I know the folks at Peacemaker Ministries have given a lot of thought to these things, so if you are interested in really working on this subject I suggest looking at the work of Ken Sande.[1] My field of ministry has especially been in the area of racial reconciliation, which has its own dynamics of inter-racial communication and cultural conflicts.

One of the constants of pastoral ministry is grieving because there will be losses along the way. Some of these losses will be from people who abandon the church, and thus abandon you. Friendships that had seemed firmly established can end suddenly, and people who were in a Bible study with you for years, always over at your house, people with whom you shared family vacations, suddenly never speak with you again. Your wife will especially bear this grief, and it will be hard for her. Much of the emotional burden for pastors and their wives is dealing with loss, which is what grief is about.

Another constant is criticism, and again your wife can bear this disproportionately. It is very hard when people feel free to criticize her, directly or indirectly. Some church people will criticize her performance as a wife and mother, or her activity or non-activity in the church. People will test your confidentiality by asking her seemingly innocent questions to see if you have told her about their issues.

On top of direct attacks against her will be attacks against you as the pastor, and some wives take any attack against their husband very personally. You cannot protect her from everything, but be careful what you bring home as you seek the support of your closest confidante and ally. Try to protect her from thinking she has to defend you and make sure neither she nor you are a gossip.

Some of the criticism you will bear has to do with your performance as a preacher, as a leader, as an administrator, as a visitor to their homes, as a responder to their needs. Your public skills and gifts are on display, and you should try to learn from these criticisms because some of them will be accurate and true. Some criticisms you will realize are a cover for other motives or problems. There is no perfect pastor, no matter what people might say about the man who pastored them prior to your arrival.

However, there is a point in which you need to ask the people to accept you as you are, with your various deficiencies, as you learn to live with each other. If you can't win their acceptance, the pastoral relationship will probably come to an end, in some way or another.

Our elders tried to have a retreat once a year. Sometimes I would pick a book and ask everyone to read it in preparation for our time together. Once we decided to take on Rick Warren's *The Purpose Driven Church*,[2] and we learned a lot from it. We decided that moving forward we would review some of the questions he posed at the end of each chapter for a discussion about how the ministry of our church was progressing, or not. So over the next few months, we ended our meetings with an analysis of our church by reviewing those questions.

As the questions were asked, it seemed like some of the elders were bothered that we hadn't made any progress about the issues which had been raised the month before, or that we were identifying even more areas of weakness. These usually pointed directly to me as the pastor. I would come home from these elder meetings annoyed and depressed. I began to realize that our focus on all the areas in which we were deficient was blinding us to the reality of our success. The church was actually doing very well. People were coming, the worship was great, and ministries were making an impact. Finally I asked the elders, "Do you think we are failing as a church or succeeding?" I told them how all of this self-examination was making me feel and did they really want to continue down this path?

Thankfully, every one of them thought our church was not only healthy but in some ways doing fantastic things. Not many churches were so cross-cultural or working among the poor, and growing, and happy. So we agreed to stop getting angry at each other about all our areas of weakness. The deficiencies were surely there, but that was not all that was there. These men were my friends, but many of us, especially as men, can be incredibly analytical and critical and do damage to relationships that we do not intend. Our efforts at self-criticism had backfired. I still believe in good evaluation, but it is important not to let our perfectionism drive us into the ground.

I heard in seminary and from other pastors that a pastor could not really make close friends in his own church. I will speak more about this idea later when we discuss the life of the pastor, but I didn't find this to be true and in fact experienced just the opposite. I believe pastors can have dear and close friends in their own churches. None of us knows the future of relationship. So it is possible that some of your closest relationships with fellow believers who share your historic struggle to build and grow the church might abandon you. If it happened to the Apostle Paul, it can happen to us. However, I do not think it is healthy to simply engage in protecting yourself and your family by being emotionally closed, protective, and acting invulnerable. Let the Lord be your hiding place. It is always safe under the shadow of the Almighty.

Conflict is inevitable, especially in ministry. Some fights you cannot dodge. If the nature of pastoral ministry is one in which you must preach, lead, and engage with the flock as a whole, or in the flock with individual sheep, then sooner or later someone is going to have a problem with you. It may be a totally imagined problem on their part. You may simply be a symbol of authority, or they may have "daddy" issues, but be assured that conflict will come! Sometimes you will be at fault. It might be a fight you started, and you may be right about the issue but went about it in the wrong way. My point here is that conflict will come because James 3:3–12 teaches us that no one can control the tongue, and you have one, either in your mouth or through what you write.

Conflict is not always bad, for there are some battles you will need to fight. If we are to *"correct, rebuke, and encourage..."* (2 Tim. 4:2), it is going to cause conflict, even if you do it with *"great patience and careful instruction."* On the other hand, if you are someone who loves to quarrel, if you love to correct others and straighten them out, or if you are contentious, then there is a good chance you don't belong in the ministry at all (2 Tim. 2:23–26).

However, our call is one in which we are called to declare God's Word, and we have to call sin—sin! Often people take that kind of thing personally. If we fail to stand for what is true, right, and good, then we are cowards. Sometimes it comes down to the choice of either pursuing the conflict or losing a whole church to evil and discord, and that we cannot allow. One specific thing that must be confronted is gossip, and sometimes we have to do that head on.

We need some Gospel and spiritual preparation for dealing with conflict. It is important that as believers, and especially as pastors, we make some preparation for the conflicts that are to come. One of the key words to remember when it comes to conflict is the word "identity." Identity is a tool that can be used by either side in spiritual warfare, especially where it becomes exposed or threatened (and made tender) in interpersonal conflict. Our identity in Christ is a marvelous protection for our hearts when we enter into conflict. If you don't know who you are in Christ, you will inevitably fall into ego competition with your antagonist. Remember who you are in Christ, and that nothing can separate you from the love of God in Christ Jesus our Lord.

People pleasing is exactly the opposite of your mission. We are called to please God, and loving people pleases him. Attempting to keep people happy and mollified is not the same as loving them. How can we disciple people in the faith if we never gently tell them the truth about areas they need to address and change? I take courage from Paul's comments in 1 Thessalonians 2:4–6: *"We are not trying to please men but God, who tests our hearts. You know we never used flattery, nor did we put on a mask to cover up greed—God is our witness. We were not looking for praise from men, not from you or anyone else."* Enough of glad-handing and plastic smiles and tiptoeing around touchy leaders and those who contribute large tithes and offerings. Be genuine and loving, but tell the truth! (See suggestions at the end of this chapter for more ideas on conflict resolution.)

---

1. Ken Sande, *The Peacemaker: A Biblical Guide to Resolving Personal Conflict*, 3rd ed. (Grand Rapids, MI: Baker, 2004); Ken Sande with Tom Raabe, *Peacemaking for Families: A Biblical Guide to Managing Conflict in Your Home* (Colorado Springs, CO: Focus on the Family, 2002); Kevin Sande and Kevin Johnson, *Resolving Everyday Conflict* (Grand Rapids, MI: Baker, 2015).

2. Rick Warren, *The Purpose Driven Church: Growth Without Compromising Your Message and Mission* (Grand Rapids, MI: Zondervan, 1995).

COUNSELING

"Why are you so buckled over, deep down?"
—Song by James Ward, from Psalm 42

People come to pastors for good counseling. Not all pastors are equally skilled in this competency. Some pastors have been well trained, while others have received hardly any training at all. Not only does training and giftedness vary among pastors, but so do their views on who should counsel believers. Some have a bias (or conviction) toward strictly biblical counseling and don't think secular counselors are qualified to help their people. On the other hand, some pastors suspect the competency of Christian counseling services. Some pastors are opposed to the field of secular psychologists and psychiatrists, even if the therapist is a Christian, as they may use secular techniques or counseling philosophies.

At the beginning of this book, I wrote about wolves in sheep's clothing. Counseling is one of those areas where some pastors get in trouble, and this comes in the guise of taking emotional advantage of someone coming to the pastor for spiritual help. God forbid any of us should sexually abuse someone coming to us, yet it has happened. If you are tempted toward such behavior, get out of that situation fast. Run, and don't worry about shutting the door behind you.

Some states have made this kind of abuse against the law, even if the adult person you are counseling consents. A pastor is a person of power, and counseling moments make people emotionally vulnerable. We must not take advantage of them. The pastor might be emotionally vulnerable in his feeling of sympathy. This must not happen, and there is no excuse for it, no matter how some counselor might seek to justify a method of comfort or distraction.

It is important for a pastor to have a grasp of his own philosophy about counseling in general, and his own counseling ministry in particular, so he can be consistent and know how he wants or intends to serve his people. Pastors should not think it strange that some members assume their pastor would have wisdom to help them through difficult moments of life. Let me start this discussion by giving my personal views on the subject.

Believers seek (and need to receive) good and wise counsel. Church members seek wisdom about school choices, vocational choices, and marriage choices. Church members have been sinned against and sin against others. This brings up problems of trauma, guilt, shame, anger, and hatred. Almost any kind of human dilemma and quest for wisdom, deliverance, comfort, and guidance is in our churches. Counsel can and does come from various sources and levels of wisdom, some good and some not so good.

First, there is the counsel internally from the Holy Spirit, which every believer has dwelling inside. Second, the Holy Spirit uses the Scripture, which every believer can read, study, and sit under its teaching. Third, there is the counsel of friends and family. We love our friends because they are usually sincere and earnest in trying to help us. The earnest counsel of a friend is one of the things that qualifies someone as a real friend (Prov. 27:9). Fourth is the counsel of community, especially in the church, where the believer is able to get a multitude of opinions and find wisdom (Prov. 11:14). Even in and from the church community, opinions need to be sifted through Scripture. The quality of counsel from people who do not have a biblical standard or an accurate biblical interpretation is something believers need to be trained to evaluate, as some might be good counsel and some might not.

Christians should not take all such extra-biblical counsel as God's truth, even if well meant. Unfortunately, sometimes friends and church members can give damaging and harmful advice. We will not even discuss here the advice that comes from media or media personalities from which many people receive their guidance.

When it comes to receiving counsel, we are assuming sanity on the part of the recipient. In order to evaluate and profit from counsel, the believer must be able to humble himself or herself and listen, have the willingness to hear and heed the voice of the Holy Spirit, and to examine guidance received through the grid of Holy Scripture.

As a pastor I believe good preaching can and should be preventative counseling. In my experience, many issues have been solved as people listen with faith to the preaching of the Gospel and the Word of God. This requires that preachers preach from the Bible about real human issues and then help the people know how to apply the truth they have heard. But I do not assume that preaching is sufficient to solve all counseling needs in the minds and hearts of people.

While pastors do not have the same amount of time available to counsel or the same expertise as therapists, it is crucial that when pastors do counsel they learn to listen to their people with humility. It is foolish to jump in with a solution too quickly. Many times I have agreed to give someone an hour, and only in the last five minutes did he or she get around to telling me what the real problem might be. Most of the time that delay was not an accident. Often the person was too ashamed or embarrassed to get to the issue and dreaded how I might react or what I would say in response.

One young woman, who I loved very much and who had been an important part of our church in her youth, came to see me one day. She had moved away and now some years later had returned to the church. As we began to talk, she told me of things that had happened to her while she was gone, and it seemed as if she was building up the courage to get to what was troubling her.

At last she told me she had become sexually involved with someone when she had moved away. I know as a pastor that people are often ashamed to tell me such things. Then she told me she had an abortion, and she knew how I had preached against abortion and stood against it. I could see the grief in her face, and I was feeling her hurt in my heart as well. I was trying to point her to forgiveness and the Gospel, but she wasn't finished telling her story. She told me she had a second abortion, and by now she was conveying in her conversation that she was emotionally crushed.

As I tried to get back to hope and mercy from God, she cried out in tears and anguish, "Oh pastor, I had a third abortion."

Sometimes I remember why I hate the devil.

I was crying with her, and I cry again as I remember that moment. My dear sister has gone on to heaven (and I believe her repentance was real), but it had taken some years for her to unload all of this to me. I have no doubt that the struggle of that guilt and disappointment (and the disappointment was intense because she was never able to have a child, for which she deeply longed) could take lots of work with a skilled and gentle therapist to overcome. My point is that healing takes time, and it even takes time to get to the beginning of healing, which is to get to the point where you can confess why you need it.

For many people the pastor represents God. For others he is the authority figure that reminds them of their parents. Too many of my members would rather hide their sins from me than ever confess directly to me. They want me to think well of them, and they actually want to keep coming to church and not always be thinking "he knows the truth about me."

They should relax. I am a Calvinist and think the worst of everyone. I am being a bit facetious, but not totally. I do believe in total depravity, and I assume everyone has past and present sin and has the potential to sin again. I know this about myself as well. I am not above judging people, but one can't be a good counselor if all he or she does is condemn people.

This means I should never despise anyone, though certainly many sins might disgust me. I am a sinner and that fact presents itself whenever I come before God's holy presence to pray. I ask Jesus to forgive me each time I call on him. I do this with confidence, because I absolutely believe in forgiveness, redemption, atonement, and not just a second chance, but a thousand chances to get back up and try again. My people should assume I expect them to have failures, even deeply shaming moral failures. I also expect them to repent and throw themselves on God's mercy and not spend the rest of their lives walking around in shame.

Good preaching often produces people looking for more direction or feeling a need to speak with someone about heart issues. When some of these issues are presented, I have realized that some people need long-term counseling. They need to talk with someone about inner struggles, feelings, troubled thinking, issues of the past, traumatic experiences, and conflicts of the present. As a pastor I had little time to be committed to just a few individuals or couples over a long period of time for intense counseling. I felt it best to refer many to a Christian professional counselor.

I always felt it my responsibility to respond to any of my members who needed counseling, and to non-members as I had time. I knew that I could try to provide counseling based on Scripture, and it would usually be directive, as the Bible often tells us what to do no matter how we feel about our circumstances. I would encourage faith, repentance, humility, love, and biblical action to solve problems.

I am not a therapist. I don't have the education or training to psychoanalyze people or to know what impact their childhood had on their present. Nor did I have the time, patience, or skills to simply listen, listen again, and listen some more, without moving to solve a problem by applying the Word of God. At the same time, I know that far too often pastors have used Bible verses like aspirin, "Take two verses and call me in two weeks." Some people need time to begin to express their fears and worries. They need skilled help to even articulate the questions in their hearts.

I believe family systems, traumatic experiences, culture, and the personal experience of sin (whether their acts of sin or the sins of others against them) affects people, their thinking and feelings. These things often act as set-ups that the devil uses to tempt people into sinful responses to internal pain. In other words, it is not just their behavior that is at issue but how they have been sinned against and what other factors have influenced them to get into their present conditions. These factors might include their social context, biological factors, psychology, and spiritual condition.

To help me in my counseling, I have sought and used information from any and all sources. I do accept the idea of common grace and realize that the Lord has given the human race amazing skills in analyzing human behavior. As far as I have been able, I have tried to analyze any knowledge and information that I have gained by sifting it through the final standard of truth, the Bible.

The field of psychology has a lot to offer pastors in understanding patterns in personality and human behavior. I believe there is such a thing as mental illness. I remember being at the Menninger Clinic in Kansas for the Army's Psychiatry Seminar and Suicide Prevention course. Dr. Menninger spoke to us Army chaplains and told us that even mentally ill people need pastors. I learned that some problems are issues of the brain and some are issues of the mind and heart.

When someone comes into my office and show signs of schizophrenia, or bipolar disorder, or tells me they are caught up in suicidal ideation, then I know I need help beyond my expertise. Sometimes people need medicine so we can actually have a reasonable conversation about how they are going to live for Jesus in the midst of their mental illness.

There is such a thing as clinical depression, and Bible study with me might help a little, but I will encourage them to see a physician as well. When marriages are falling apart and one spouse has a mental illness, it is not enough for a pastor to simply tell the other spouse to love or submit to their mentally ill spouse, though they certainly should as much as they are able. However, what good does it do allowing people to live in guilt about something which is not really their fault or that they, using only their positive behavior, are helpless to change.

If you ask me, "So then, you implicitly believe in secular psychiatry and trust everything they say?" Of course not! Many in the field of psychiatry can't seem to agree with each other, nor do some of the things they teach agree with Scripture. I am appalled at how inconsistent much of secular psychology is and how so much of diagnosis and prescription for drugs that deal with psychotic episodes seem to be a crap shoot. Many patients I have known have had to endure a lot of trial and error with prescriptions before they became stable.

Yet notwithstanding all the problems in the fields of psychology and mental health, I am deeply grateful for the study of the human mind, brain chemistry, behavior, and counseling techniques. Inept and confusing diagnoses do not invalidate the idea that a person might have a chemical imbalance in the body and that there may be a medicine that might help keep them stable. Meeting with me won't be enough to change them. I need the help of mental health professionals, and though I realize that they are not all of the same quality (as is true with pastors too), I am grateful for their help.

People with emotional and psychological illness can still sin. Excusing or enabling sinful behavior doesn't help to relieve them or protect them from the consequences of their actions, though many of us try. Helping those with mental illness to work toward personal responsibility is important. Consequences for destructive behavior are usually drastic and fairly inescapable—the loss of reputation, job, home, family, and even life. Members with mental illness still need to be enfolded into the life and ministry of the church and not treated as lepers or untouchables.

At our congregation, we have had to call the police during worship services a few times because of people who were having manic or psychotic episodes because they decided that they no longer needed to take their medicine. Pastoring families whose loved ones have such drastic mental illness is hard, often confusing, but so very necessary.

I have tried to lead my church into helping to provide funds for members who can't afford professional counseling on their own, especially when we refer them to Christian counselors. We think it is important for the dignity of people for them to pay something for their own healing, but we realize they can't or won't keep going if they can't afford the fee.

Counseling services (especially if the church pays for it) are not a way for a member to avoid church discipline. Church discipline is a means to reclaim sinners, and it begins simply with member-to-member accountability. Counselors should be able to interact with pastors about holding members accountable to their vows for holy living. In order to do that a pastor, at the beginning of therapy, should obtain written consent from the counselee so that information obtained from the therapist doing the counseling can be shared with the pastor and session.

One of the realities of medical economics in our country is that pastors are going to have people in their church that have inadequate medical insurance for the treatment of mental illness. Some pastors will have parents in their congregation who have an adult child who lives with them but has severe mental illness. They will become caught up in the merry-go-round of calling the police or mental health services, having their child held for seventy-two hours and then released back in their home. Sometimes the person returning home has not been properly medicated. Sometimes they are furious with being sent away again to a psychiatric emergency room. Quite often the insurance money runs out after a specified number of days, and the family is terrorized in their own home with threats of violence or aberrant behavior.

Many pastors simply stay away from these situations. They feel helpless against the mental illness. I have certainly felt helpless at times. There are pastors who try to keep showing up to comfort and pray with and for the caregivers. Some pastors will eventually face a family tragedy and have to perform funerals for the suicide or homicide victim. They try to comfort parents struggling with grief, shame, and guilt for some horrible thing their grown child has done. There will be pastoral care and counseling needed surrounding such situations, even if the pastor cannot cure the person with the illness.

There are physicians who come to the end of their skills in treating a patient. Some doctors have been known to write off a patient when they can no longer help. They do not refer to someone more skilled, or even continue a relationship with that person. Unfortunately pastors can fall into this as well. If we cannot "fix" a person we might not like the feeling of failure it gives us. I wonder: How long will it take us as pastors to realize fixing people is not our business and not in our capacity in the first place?

People with mental illness and deep psychological problems need the love of God and the faithfulness of God's people, but it is hard to stick with them both as shepherds and as the family of God since it strains resources and is so confusing. Sometimes one of the only victories we as a congregation might be able to have in such situations is that we stood with a person and a family, and we were faithful to love them somehow.

CRISES

Sometimes the counsel a pastor must give comes at a moment of crisis. In these moments it is not therapy that is being sought, but wisdom and solutions. One of the most heart-wrenching moments comes near the end of someone's life. Much has been written in medical ethics about the continuation of life by mechanical means and respirators. Doctors and hospitals stress having advance directives and living wills. I think good pastors need to encourage their congregations to think about these things. At one time I tried to interview every family and ask them what their desires were about such things, even about funeral plans. If a church has a good way to keep copies of these interviews, I highly recommend it.

Inevitably people will face these issues as families, and they will be unprepared. Families can become divided; some want to keep hope alive. They don't want to do anything that would allow their loved one to slip away. Other family members will advocate for "pulling the plug," often in the name of mercy or because they believe their loved one would not want to be sustained in the present state.

This is often exactly the moment the pastor arrives in the ICU or the emergency room. It might be an auto accident, the drowning of a child, a suicide attempt, a fall from a cliff, or some kind of sudden stroke or heart attack, and people are not ready to say goodbye to their loved one. Therapy may be needed later to recover from the grief and anger this moment will create, but church members often want a word from heaven or at least of spiritual wisdom at this point.

The pastor should gather them for prayer or bring in the elders for prayer. Sometimes the pastor has to be an intermediary between the doctors or hospital staff and explain things to either side. Some doctors are surprised of course to discover that families find a pastor's authority to be greater than that of the doctors, and that has a lot to do with relationship, history, and personal respect.

Pastors need to seek experience in hospital ministry if for no other reason than to learn skills and language for these critical moments of possible life-ending decisions. Many doctors are relieved to turn over a grieving family member to the arms of a pastor. But pastors should never be presumptuous about such decisions. If the pastor has not heard from the person who might be dying, or known their desires, and has no written record of such, it is not his place to call for the end of life. He can help the family think and pray it through. He can help the family discuss it, but he cannot lead at this moment. He must only love, support, and answer biblical questions.

Pre-counseling families about their future funerals is important, for them, for the church, and for the sake of the Gospel. Here is one important truth some of our church members don't realize. Once they die, someone else in their family will make all the decisions about the funeral, burial, or memorial service. This will not be decided by the pastor or the church, unless prior instructions have been given. I think Christian funerals and preaching the Gospel at funerals is very important, and I want my members to plan for such and not have an unbelieving family member deprive them of it.

Thankfully most church members are usually going to have less drastic issues that will not call for visits to hospitals or prison. Yet their normal issues are very real, and some of those issues push people to affairs, divorce, anger, internal bitterness, terrible insecurities, destructive behavior, and overcompensation in various ways. It will take a discerning pastor to see all the clues and marks of a life about to fall apart and then learn when and how to intervene. Pastors can sometimes be fatalistic, just waiting for sin to come out in the open and then rebuke it. Or they can proactively love people, listen, and seek to have hearts opened and exposed so the sweet balm of the Gospel can be applied. If there is a sense of deeper need, people should be referred to good counselors so that long-term care can be given.

It would be wise for pastors to learn the various resources they have in their own congregation or in the broader Christian community. They should learn where to find effective counseling (not all are equal in their abilities). Congregations should be aware of curricula that small groups can study so they can address specific emotional and spiritual issues. There are various training courses available to make church members better lay counselors and to at least become aware of various struggles people go through. The list of potential issues is huge. Most pastors will admit they don't know how to deal with all of them.

One of the greatest lessons I learned in my times of counseling was to realize I was insufficient for this task, both in knowledge and in skill. The times when I was presumptuous and thought I had the answers were probably my worst times of counseling. As people who needed counseling walked into my office, I learned to pray, "Lord, I know I can't fix this person, and don't even know how to help them, so I throw myself on you. Please give me some wisdom to help them." I learned that God does give wisdom when we ask him for it (see James 1:5). Sometimes that wisdom was to say, "And here is a number you should call."

VISITATION

You know that I have not hesitated to preach anything that would be helpful to you but have taught you publicly and from house to house.
Acts. 20:20

Visiting members is one area in which I not only felt insufficient, but sometimes downright guilty. There were times the issue was my own laziness, my own desire for time alone, or the desire to be in my own house and not in the house of a member.

In pastoral work the people hear and see the pastor more than he actually gets to hear from them. The people begin to feel close to their pastor as they listen to his sermons each Sunday. In the preaching moments, church members hear his stories, learn about his growing up and background, his love and admiration for various authors. They hear stories about his wife and children and the personal details he shares. At the same time, the pastor might know very little about specific individuals in the church, and how could he unless he spends time with them? Preaching to your people is not the same thing as spending time with them.

The people in a congregation who have the most emergencies or crisis moments in their lives, or the most anguish in their personal lives, often become those who will get most of the pastor's attention. If you have a strong spiritual life, are faithful in attendance, or have few if any disasters (whether they be spiritual or physical), then you most likely will not get to spend a lot of time pouring out your life story to the pastor. He will not necessarily know about your extended family, not know how intensely you feel about theological, political, or congregational things unless one of you makes the effort to get to know each other. The pastor will probably not get to all of your family celebrations, graduations, etc. If the church is large and growing, he just will not have the time.

Each pastor has to develop a strategy about how he is going to care for his flock, how he is going to get to know them, how he is going to pursue them. As the church grows, this often develops from a personal relationship and intimacy to a delegated one through small groups or associate pastors, or elder-shepherd groups. There are many people who want to be on a first-name basis with the pastor or who want to have regular meetings or check-ins with their pastor, but this will most likely be especially true for congregational leaders and officers.

There have been pastors who made the effort to make a home visit to each and every member family once per year, which then extended to maybe every other year as the church grew. There are church members who make the effort to invite the pastor and his wife over for a meal at their home. I am sure there were people in my congregation who were surprised that I never came to their home. I have also been amazed that many of my members never once in decades invited me to their home, although there have been many occasions when my wife invited the whole church to our home at various times of the year. I was sometimes shameless in advertising that if we were invited over for a meal, we would come.

I am not upset with them for not inviting me to their home. I actually didn't expect them to do that. I felt the mandate was on me to pursue my people and not on them to pursue me. As I have mentioned, I often felt guilty that I could not visit everyone, nor be at many significant moments of their lives. I am thankful that I have tried to live in the power, joy, and freedom of the Gospel or else I don't think I could ever have stood all the feelings of failure inside me for not being all or doing all that I should have done as a pastor. I believe this is a very real emotional burden for many pastors.

However, I have tried to make opportunities to actually get to know my members. Sometimes this has come from crisis moments, and I have spent a lot of time with certain of my people in those times. Sometimes this has come from happy family moments, such as weddings. Sometimes this has come from ministry involvement where we have served together, whether from one-day or weekend training events, or mission trips, and sometimes through retreats or camps. One church retreat can have more impact on relationships than a whole year of church services.

Sometimes I have been to the workplace of my people, especially when I have been invited to a ceremony or special event. This has certainly made me feel they wanted me in their lives. I have made it through many days on the free lunches provided by members who wanted to spend time with me.

The visiting of people in hospitals, in prison, and with families at funeral homes or a wake are important opportunities for extending pastoral care. Besides that, it is a biblical mandate (Matt. 25:39–40). It is possible for a pastor to develop a deeper and faster relationship with his people during times of emergency or death than at any other time. People will remember the pastor who shows up, but those who do not will be remembered in a different way.

One of the worst things to happen to a pastor is to delay getting to the emergency room, or the hospital room, or to hospice, and then find out the person they wanted and needed to see has passed away. Of course things can happen fast, pastors can be out of town, they can be engaged in a scheduled meeting and plan to get there as soon as possible but not make it in time. It is really helpful for pastors to have staff, or elders, or deacons, who take on the responsibility of making sure the pastor remembers who needs seeing and keeps reminding him. It is even better when elders or deacons tell the pastor they will come and get him and go with him.

One of the obstacles to a pastor getting out in the evenings to visit in the homes of his people is that he might actually like to spend time with his own family. It is also true that many families with children are caught up in a vast amount of school or after school events and have little time to be caught at home. Though there are lots of difficulties in achieving it, each pastor has to pursue his people, get to know them, listen to them, and pray for them. It is not enough simply to wait for people to make appointments to come and see you in your office. This might be more efficient for the pastor's time, but the job is not about us but about them—the sheep, the Lord's people.

Since we live in an age of telecommunications, a phone call or text can be a blessing to someone. It's important to know someone actually cares. The pastor might have to do this representationally through his officers, staff, and small group leaders, but he must lead in the example of getting to know and relate to people.

It is crazy to think some pastors that can just be unfriendly. It is one thing to be an introvert and another to be unfriendly. It is one thing to be limited in the time you have available to hang out with your members and another to purposefully limit your time. I wonder how many pastors analyze the amount of time they have available for the wealthy in their church versus the time spent with average folks?

I have shown up unannounced at homes and had to wait outside while they put all the gambling and drinking paraphernalia away. I realized then that my presence could intimidate and shame people, when I had no intention or desire to.

It is helpful to call first when you want to make a home visit if that is possible. I wish I could give pastors a secret formula to make visiting easier, but I don't have one. I can only tell you that those people in my church seemed to greatly appreciate the time I spent with them, whether it was planned or spontaneous. I only wish I could have done it more for more of them.

WEDDINGS

And the day of death better than the day of birth. It is better to go to a house of mourning than to go to a house of feasting, for death is the destiny of every man; the living should take this to heart.
Ecclesiastes 7:1–2

Pastors have the humbling privilege of ministering to people at some of the most significant moments in their lives: weddings and funerals. You can only effectively pastor people who let you pastor them, and these events, especially if done well, earn you that right.

Weddings are supposed to be fun and joyous, and it is important that you as a pastor don't mess up this very special day for the new couple. The whole prospect of people coming to you to ask you to marry them is an honor, but it can be problematic. There are some people you should not marry to each other, and saying so will make you appear to be judgmental or even bigoted. Preparing for a pastoral ministry means each pastor has to have a pastoral philosophy about marriage and policies about who he will marry and what he requires of the couple in order to do it. It is best to be clear on these before you are asked.

You may be in a denomination or congregation that already has standards or policies concerning marriage, including remarriage for those who have been divorced. Young pastors may think these decisions will be easy, but sooner or later there will be a call on their conscience and integrity, and what should be a happy event may become a troubled one.

Before we get into the controversial issues, let me say that pastors should have a goal to officiate weddings ceremonies where the Gospel is preached, where marriage is celebrated and endorsed, and where the community (especially that of the church) gets behind this new couple. The pastor is not the center of the event, although he plays a significant part. Pastors can selfishly seek to be the center of attention and rob glory from Jesus and the bride, neither of which is warranted.

Pastors can preach way too long at a wedding, and I can almost guarantee that most people there will forget everything you said, but they won't forget that you were boring and distracting. Weddings are great moments for teaching what marriage is about, but pastors need to be careful to not get into a long-winded discourse covering all the things the couple should have been taught in premarital counseling. Nor should pastors fall into the trap about preaching against all the attacks on biblical marriage, from homosexuality to divorce. I have heard sermons at weddings and felt terrible for the couple and sorry for myself that I had to endure it.

A couple might come to you and ask you to officiate at their wedding. The first question for me is: Are they qualified to be married? There are several layers to this question. In my conscience, as far as I understand the Bible, I cannot marry a Christian to a non-Christian. Also, is one of the parties still married to someone else? You might think this is a stupid question, but it can be a problem. If they have been previously married, was the divorce not only finalized, but was it enacted for biblical reasons? Are they emotionally, financially, and mentally prepared for what they are getting themselves into?

I reserve the right to say no to any couple for all kinds of reasons. I try to tell every couple that if after counseling them I feel they are not ready, qualified, equipped, or prepared I will refuse to do the ceremony. I am ordained by the church of Jesus Christ, not the state. As a pastor I am responsible to my denomination and to my own conscience to maintain the standards of godly marriage. I am one of the gatekeepers, and those standards are to protect both couples and society.

I am fully aware that couples don't need me to marry them. There are lots of options for them, whether it be a pastor of another church, justice of the peace, or certified officiant. None of that excuses me if I perform a legally binding marriage ceremony for a couple that I think has no business getting married right then.

I have refused some couples, and there were others I should have refused. At a certain point in my ministry I was challenged to sign my name to a pledge that I would never marry a couple that had not had premarital counseling. I did so and have never regretted it. It has protected me from demands for an emergency or sudden ceremony. Couples that tell you they will be willing to go through counseling after the ceremony don't always follow through. In our county in Tennessee (Hamilton County), couples receive a discount on their marriage license if they can apply for it with a document certifying that they have received premarital counseling. This incentive has apparently helped cut down on the divorce rate in our area, along with the demand that couples with children seeking a divorce must have some counseling before a divorce will be awarded.

I am willing to marry two non-Christians, but I still require counseling. Once I had a couple come to me because they knew I was an Army chaplain. They informed me that neither of them were a professing Christian, but I told them I would require counseling and my counseling was Christian in content. They agreed to endure it. The bride stipulated however that she did not want the word "obey" in the vows. So we proceeded, and I gave them what I give to every couple, teaching from the Bible about Christ and his church and how a husband and wife are to respect and love each other.

On the day of the wedding I honestly forgot about her asking me not to use the word "obey" in the vows. When I spoke that word, the eyes of the bride grew wide, and she glared at me for several moments. Only then did it hit me. She finally said, "I do!" I had made a mistake. I wasn't trying to trick her, and I felt bad. I had hoped they would become Christians during the counseling sessions, but that hadn't happened. The celebration finished, and I didn't hear from them again.

Until one night, a year or so later, when I received a phone call from that bride. She told me her husband, a soldier, was being deployed for Operation Desert Storm. I was being deployed there too. The woman told me that both she and her husband had become Christians. She wanted me to know and asked me to pray for her husband. I was so glad to get that phone call! Though there is not always a happy ending, we must not compromise our standards in order to please a couple that wants to get married.

There are many counseling courses and computerized compatibility tests. Each pastor should decide what he thinks is adequate and what is necessary for preparation. Some pastors seem to give a college-level, semester-long course in marriage and family. That is fine if you have the time, but nothing except the grace of God will absolutely guarantee the permanence of a marriage. Yet there should be a minimum of instruction with solid content. My teaching included the roles of husband and wife, communication and how to have a "good" argument, budgeting and money, sex, and general guidance on families of origin, friends, and decision-making. Those who have grown up in a home where healthy marriage was modeled have a definite advantage.

I have had women tell me they have found a man they want to

marry, but there is one problem... "he is not a Christian." Sometimes they burst into tears before I can even give my answer. I say, "You know what I am going to say. I have said it from the pulpit. What did you expect me to say?" But I almost always tell them, "I will give you premarital counseling, if he will submit to it. Maybe he will get saved before the day comes." Hallelujah, this has happened several times! I baptized one man at his wedding, and others have become officers in my church.

I have had people get angry at me because I refused to marry them. Some were previously married, not just one time but several. I made it a personal policy that I would not perform a wedding for anyone who had more than one previous marriage. After one refusal, a couple was married by another pastor in our church and then later they divorced. Once they were married, I supported that marriage and didn't like it when they referred to my refusal by saying, "We should never have gotten married in the first place." That's right, they should not have gotten married, but once done it should stay done.

You may have families who have been in the church a long time, and one of their children wants to marry outside of the faith. Pressure is brought to bear from these long-time financial supporters of the church. Surely an exception will be made for this church family so their children can be married by the pastor in their own church? No. Consistent teaching on this from the pulpit can guard you from this kind of conflict.

I have made lots of mistakes in performing weddings. I'm trying to forget them, so I won't mention them here. Please, may all those embarrassed or angry couples forgive me! But usually I have had a great time with the couples and their families. I try to make my wedding homily short, joyful, and convicting. I always try to articulate the Gospel. A few times I have had to confess (by prior agreement) that the couple is pregnant but that they have repented and are right with God and the church. This has made some in-laws want to kill me.

It is really good to have the names of the couple written in your notes or to have the program before you. It is amazing how my mind can go blank right at the moment I am supposed to introduce them as a couple. I have learned to relax and not get so uptight about getting everything right. "Whatever happens," I tell the couple, "we will pronounce you husband and wife, so don't sweat it." Of course, some families (especially the brides') have imagined this moment for a long time. Sometimes the effort to get every detail correct takes a lot of the joy out of the day. I say, make it a party!

FUNERALS

The book of Ecclesiastes says in 7:2, *"It is better to go to a house of mourning than to go to a house of feasting, for death is the destiny of every man; the living should take this to heart."* Funerals are one of the most important events in a family's life. They are strategic moments for pastors and should neither be avoided nor treated as an interruption to ministry. This is where the Gospel should be boldly preached.

In terms of reaching one's community or neighborhood, sometimes neighborhood families have no home church or pastor. If they realize you care about them, they might ask you to handle the service. Usually they find out that you care because you have been to the hospital or home when bad news came. I encourage pastors to take advantage of this great opportunity to love on families. Your congregation should be prepared to help any family with funerals or repasts (the meal after the funeral). Being prepared means that church members need to know that sometimes they will have to respond on short notice, and the church treasurer needs to know that sometimes it is necessary for the church to help pay for the funeral.

Some churches have policies stating that only members can have a funeral in the church building. If you are the pastor in such a church, you should still demand freedom from your elders to be available to do funerals at a funeral home or another church, even for non-Christians. But it is my strong recommendation that churches use their buildings for funerals. It is a representation that this person has died in the Lord. I don't have any problem having a funeral for a non-Christian in the church building because it usually means that people are going to hear me preach who might never have otherwise.

My pastor growing up told me he never took money from church members for weddings or funerals. I have tried to practice this, but have had many families seek to give me a gratuity for my work. I have told them up front not to worry about it and would refuse it if I ever felt this couple or family didn't have any money to spare, especially if they were members who paid my salary anyway. There is no sense getting in arguments with people over it, so if they insist I take it.

If couples outside the church wish my time for counseling and a ceremony, I am happy to accept a gift for my time, and I think it right for them to offer it. I have never "charged" for a funeral. Usually it works the other way around, with our church helping to pay for the funeral, or for the food at a repast, with our folks doing the work of setting everything up.

I give glory to God and thanks to the congregation at New City Fellowship for hosting some of the greatest funerals I have ever experienced. Though that sounds strange, people who have attended some of our funerals and who were not part of our congregation have told me that when they die they hope that New City will do their funerals.

We might host someone's funeral if their family needed us to do it, but to actually do what some call a "New City Funeral," well, (the audacity of such a request) to say it simply, you have to earn it. If it's someone we loved, someone we have served with, someone we knew was a saint and has gone to heaven—that funeral is and ought to be a great event. We are grieving and rejoicing, weeping and laughing with joyful memories all at the same time. Thanks to James Ward, we almost always sing a song he wrote in the early days of our church the first time one of our members died, "Death Is Ended," to close out a member's funeral.[1] The hope and joy of that truth makes all the difference.

---

1. https://www.youtube.com/watch?v=fBHTpyoyToY

DISCIPLESHIP

Part of the challenge in a congregation is for members to be in a relationship with an older and more mature Christian, especially one that knows the vision of the church and has a burden for the growth of the person he or she is discipling. Yes, pastors have to cast vision and train and teach the people. Yet without personal interaction, vulnerability, and accountability with another Christian, it is hard to apply lessons to life as need arises.

Discipleship is friendship with a purpose, and a friendship that has more loyalty to Jesus than to the relationship. A pastor is just one person and not able to interact with every member each and every day. He has to multiply himself by encouraging believers to take on the responsibility of lovingly serving others to help them mature in their faith. Much of discipleship happens in joint engagement in ministry. It is not simply about Bible memorization or accountability meetings.

Many young adults look for a program within a church to help them establish these kinds of relationships. Pastors of smaller congregations may not have the staff to administer discipleship relationships as a program. Nevertheless, it is good for pastors to advocate the idea, to encourage people to seek someone to mentor them, to pray with and for them, to be available for counsel. It is good for pastors to encourage older believers to look for peers or younger people who might need this kind of relationship, or to volunteer their availability to the pastor in case someone wants an older believer in their life. There are books and programs available to help churches establish such relationships.

LOVING AND BEING A FUNCTIONAL
PART OF THE BODY

All the believers were one in heart and mind.
No one claimed that any of his possessions was
his own, but they shared everything they had.
Acts 4:32

My comments here are not about an administrative scheme to make church "body life" happen. However, I don't discount the value of having a strong and vibrant organizational structure to help the process along. Larger churches need someone administering and attending to the details of recruiting, engaging, and monitoring members into and along the flow of small groups and ministry groups.

Whatever plan you implement is much better than leaving members to fend for themselves. Most senior pastors need other staff to oversee this part of ministry if they want it done effectively. The plan you choose and announce is only as valuable as the attention paid to maintain it and keep it going. That is why pastors should delegate this responsibility.

Several components make a church welcoming, warm, and inviting. We can ask:

- What makes and keeps members happy to be in the church?
- What gives members a sense of belonging?
- What helps to break down barriers that keep people from becoming friends and loving their fellow members?
- What gives members the hope of growing and developing as believers?
- What gives members a sense of ownership in the church body?

Many people first come to churches because of a personal invitation; someone they know invited them. Then the worship experience and familial atmosphere hopefully encourage them to return. They come and are not unduly inconvenienced to enter and stay (place to park, place to sit, child care, and welcomed but not embarrassed). They enjoy, can follow, and engage with the worship, including the preaching. Certainly the Holy Spirit must be at work as well.

Visitors may initially return if there is a cultural connection, but they will keep coming and stay longer if there is a soul connection. In short, if their soul is blessed to be there. Some people like being anonymous in a large congregation and don't want intimacy with other members. They stay and feel connected through the charismatic pastor, the vibrant worship experience, and possibly their engagement with the church's image or reputation. Ultimately however, there must be some relationships built or these anonymous believers will float or fly to another place as soon as something makes them uncomfortable.

There is growing demand by many church attenders that attention be paid to their needs. They want more Bible studies, more fellowship groups, more help with their marriages, more support with their children and youth, more available counseling, and more how-to courses to guide them and their families through life. These desires are real and sometimes desperately needed. So how can a pastor call his people to mission if they are demanding that he focus on ministry to them?

If a pastor doesn't experience the tension and conflict between a missional focus and a ministering focus he has probably sided for only one part of a congregation's need. Many books about the church stress the primacy of preaching. Some do this because they see the role of the church diminishing in society or because they think this was the emphasis of the New Testament. But they confuse the preaching to and among the lost in the book of Acts (the history of the early church) with what they do on Sunday mornings.

Let's be done with self-indulgent congregations. As a pastor, I want my people to grow in Christ, to love each other radically, and to develop as leaders. A foundational element of this growth is to help them live for something other—and bigger—than themselves as a congregation. It is absurd for some to demand that churches not be engaged in good works or address the needs of justice and mercy lest it be a distraction from the Gospel. This sounds more like a prescription for a preacher's job security than a passion for the church, let alone a misunderstanding of the teaching and practice of the Gospel of the Kingdom.

There are lots of opinions about how central worship must be to the life of Christians, individually and corporately. Jesus tells us in John 4 that God seeks worshipers. Worship should be one of the greatest recurring events in the life of believers. There is joy and renewal in worship as we experience God's real and glorious presence. How could we possibly live as Christians without worship?

Yet how can we worship a missional God and not do missions? How can we worship a just and merciful God and not practice justice and show mercy? God tells Judah, in the face of their being religious while not caring about injustice or the poor, *"You cannot fast as you do today and expect your voice to be heard on high"* (Isa. 58:4). Much of our common worship experience is self-indulgent worship and produces selfish churches and selfish Christians.

If you want to live, then die to yourself. If you want to be great, become the least. If we had more preaching and Bible study on that topic, churches might be less popular but more flexible, radical, effective, and dynamic. If building a larger audience and maintaining it are our goals, we have failed to grasp the speed and fire of the Gospel. If you want discipleship, follow Christ and follow his disciples who are actually doing something and going somewhere and not simply producing a weekly show.

Today we wish to build churches with no sacrifice, which results in materialistic, indulgent, entertained, and entitled congregations. They give out of their abundance, not out of their essence. They rise to the challenge of bigger and better buildings, yet they fail by having small budgets for mercy and development of the poor.

Our people need each other, and they need loyal friends. They need to love and be loved. They need older believers speaking into their lives. They need leaders they can follow as models and mentors. Our people need an outside challenge so they can lift up their eyes to the harvest. They need grounding in the Word, but they also need opportunities to grow by sharing that Word with others, especially the lost.

From day one, pastors should be thinking of developing leaders. Train, train, and train your people. Give them responsibility to do ministry and the authority to do it. Delegate work to others and don't hold all of the control. Recruit, train, and encourage young people, especially teens, in ministry. Challenge them to pray about God's calling on their lives, potentially in vocational ministry. Cast great vision that includes small but crucial decisions of faithful service in the life of the body. There are many small but consistent acts of obedience on the way to glory.

The Great Commission of Christ is a glorious calling. The glory of God to be seen and realized in all parts of life and in all places in the world is a glorious challenge. When people are engaged in mission and ministry, they develop skills, grow spiritually, and bond with other believers in the work of the Lord.

SUGGESTIONS

1. To remember who you are in Christ, meditate on Romans 8. We are sons of God, and no one can take that away from us, and no one can separate us from the love of God which is in Christ Jesus our Lord.

2. Knowing the identity of our real enemy is important to keep in mind, so we realize quickly what is going on in, behind, and through the circumstances of the conflict. Ephesians Chapter 6 teaches us that we *"wrestle not against flesh and blood, but against principalities and powers, against the rulers of darkness in this world."* The Apostle Paul is speaking about the devil, and we can forget that he is the real enemy. We need great protection against the temptation to hate people and not have sympathy for them. The reality is that sometimes we can be used as Satan's instruments when we are sinful. Ministry is rife with spiritual warfare, and it is always in play. Satan is always looking for a chance to use conflict to break our unity and fellowship and to grieve the Holy Spirit of God. One clue that Satan is involved is when our opponent is

always being accused in our minds. The devil is the accuser of the brethren (Rev. 12:10).

3. Knowing the "made in God's image" identity of our human opponents is also helpful. It can keep us from making total jerks of ourselves. People are created in God's image. They belong to him as he is their master, and it is to him they will stand or fall (not us), as it says in Romans 14:4. Believers are people for whom Christ died, and nonbelievers might just be his elect who haven't realized it yet. All of them are people whom God loves and are our neighbors. These very people, the people we are having difficulty with, are the same people we are commanded to love as ourselves.

4. You must engage when church discipline is required. Some pastors seek to avoid bringing a member under discipline because it seems like the trouble is a personal conflict. If a member is slandering, gossiping, backbiting, and creating division, it must be confronted and rebuked, sometimes publicly. Learn how to follow the Rules of Discipline and learn how to apply them with grace and wisdom.

5. Failures in conflict resolution create consequences, usually bad ones. If you run away from the conflicts you should have, or start ones you shouldn't due to your anger, or handle them in an unbiblical way, they will leave bad memories and emotional scars in yourself and in other people. We are to *"seek peace and pursue it"* (Ps. 34:14, 1 Pet. 3:11). Most people recover from conflicts handled well, and in fact grow from them and gain respect for those they may have once disrespected.

6. Healthy conflict doesn't always look successful. People have pride. We don't always handle things well. It often takes time, reflection, and prayer to realize someone else was correct in what they said to us. So if

that is true for you, then give other people time and space and seek to protect their dignity. Humiliating someone, attempting to have them admit to every fault, and pushing them to give you due recognition that you were absolutely right is not the vindication you should seek. We cannot fix everyone or every situation. Sometimes the loose ends have to be left with God. Ambiguity doesn't always mean defeat.

7. We need to clarify what a successful outcome might be.

- In ourselves—that we did not sin, that we were personally willing to take the loss, and that we were and are ready to forgive and reconcile, that we have confessed our sins and admitted our fault, and that we stood for the glory of God. I have found that humility (humbling myself before others) has been one of the greatest tools for conflict resolution, when by God's grace I have been able to show it (1 Cor. 6:7).
- In others—that they have been heard, that they have been respected, that we have made an honest and clear attempt to understand their position and to clearly present ours, that they have been assured of the grace and love of God.
- In the church—that we have sought the unity and peace of the body of Christ, that we have sought the purity of the church, that we have sought the restoration of sinners, and that we have done things in an open, honest, and non-manipulative manner.

8. We should learn how conflict was handled in the Bible, and I point you to three stories that you might read and think about how the Apostle Paul handled his conflicts.

- Paul's conflict with Barnabas in Acts 15:36–41

- Paul's conflict with the Apostle Peter in Galatians 2:11–16
- Paul's desire to see conflict ended between two women in Philippians 4:2–3

9. Learn positive communication goals and skills. I end my comments with referring you to something I have recommended to couples I have counseled prior to marriage. I think Ephesians 4 could be called the communications chapter of the Bible. When you read it, look for every admonition and teaching about how to relate, react, treat, and communicate with others. Paul writes: *"Forgiving each other, even as God for Christ's sake has forgiven you"* (Eph. 4:32). Try to acquire active listening skills.

PART SIX
ECCLESIOLOGY

LOVING THE CHURCH AS THE BRIDE OF CHRIST

But everything should be done in a fitting and orderly way.
1 Corinthians 14:40

An ecclesiast is a churchman, one who works in the church, does the work of the church, and—might I add—believes in it. Pastors ought to be ecclesiasts. They should have a theology and ideology about the work and necessity of the institutional church and be loyal to it. They should know the church system they are in and how to function effectively within it. If you are the pastor of a church, then you ought to have a passion for it, defend its necessity, and stop being either a parasite that simply lives off it or an autoimmune disease within it. Pastors should certainly not be the people tearing down the church.

There are some pastors and lay Christians who take every chance they can to criticize the church. They mock it, act as if the local church is a necessary evil, and imply that they personally are above it. How can you love a bridegroom and make fun of his bride? I know that some churches are not Gospel-focused and do not honor God. I also know some churches and church members have been deeply hurt by charlatan preachers, manipulative leaders, and various kinds of spiritual or even sexual abuse. Lord have mercy on us!

Yet the church is where God's people are gathered in all their hypocrisies, in their messy sins, and also in their fellowship, love, and sacrifice for Christ and each other. Many of these critical comments about churches are attempts to convince people that Jesus is better than the church. Of course he is! The church is made up of the people that Jesus came to save because they are so messed up, not because they deserve it (1 Tim. 1:15, Luke 19:10). We don't do people any favors by adding to their cynicism about, and thus increasing their resistance to, local churches. The local church is exactly where each Christian needs to be. We need to be about the work of making each local church all that it should and could be, for good.

If you are a pastor in a church, there is some type of organizational structure. You need to know how your church and denomination functions. This applies to any church, from one with an independent single pastor with leaders he may or may not have appointed to an established church within a denomination. The more complicated the accountability structure (or hierarchy), the more organizational knowledge will be needed to function well.

In my years of pastoring, I have met pastors who take different attitudes to the system they have willingly placed themselves in. When a pastor takes the step of going on staff, whether with an independent church or joining a denomination, he does this voluntarily. Yet some speak as if they despise the system in which they must operate. Some even actively resist cooperating in the framework.

Potential pastors usually consider where they might minister, and they might sense a possibility in a denomination that attracts them. At the same time, they may be intimidated by the credentialing process and wonder whether there is a way to take short-cuts to get licensed and ordained. They also may wonder whether they need to conform to all the doctrines of the denomination.

My advice to anyone seeking to be ordained in a specific denomination, if one doctrinally agrees in good conscience, is to do the work and earn the credentialing. Usually there are alternative routes (I advocate for this), but some work still must be put into the process. Others have done it without dying (though it may feel like it) and have earned the respect of their peers with whom they work. For the sake of conscience, I would discourage anyone from trying to enter a denomination or church in which you think you have to hide your real beliefs in order to get in. God forbid you should lie just to get and hold a job in the church. That cannot possibly be a good idea.

There are many ministers who are nonconformists. They want to be ordained, and they want to pastor, but they just seem irritated by all the rules and regulations and requirements of being in a particular church government system. They don't agree with all the rules but give verbal assent in order to be part of the denomination.

On the other hand, there are those who become well-schooled in the denominational rules and laws, are astute in parliamentary process, and find joy in being able to move or hinder various pieces of church legislation. They relish using the organizational system and act like that is the real life of the church. They suggest that there could be no higher calling or better investment of their time than to know all the procedural rules and use them in church meetings. Character has a lot to do with how someone uses procedural rules in the church, so does a correct understanding of what God wants us to accomplish as his church. Jesus is the only Lord and head of the Church, and it is his glory we are to be about, not our own or that of our little power groups.

In general there are three types of church government: Congregational, Episcopal, and Presbyterian. The Congregational type is democratic, in which the congregation votes on all the important things, and it is usually built on the independence of the individual congregation. They may or may not have deacons in addition to pastors, whose authority is usually set by the rules and traditions of their own congregations. Though the church may be part of an association, it is essentially independent and not forced to obey the dictates of a higher governing authority.

Episcopal government is hierarchical and uses elevated offices (i.e., bishops) to oversee congregations, a diocese, or a region. There are free-floating bishops (usually in independent or self-appointed groups) who oversee several churches they have started or have come to an overseer for help and guidance, and there are large denominations that have a very specific way of elevating pastors to the role of bishop. The bishop usually can transfer, place, or dismiss pastors according to his judgment, subject to the rules of the denomination.

Presbyterian government is rule by elders. These elders are elected by their congregations, and represent them in a regional body known as the presbytery. These churches are usually held together by a Book of Church Order (which details how the church is supposed to function), as well as by their confessional documents (what they have agreed to believe). The pastors, also known as Teaching Elders, are members of, receive their credentials from, and are subject to the spiritual discipline of the presbytery.

Presbyterian denominations usually have a final court that convenes annually in either a General Assembly or a Synod, where judicial cases are finalized and issues of government, doctrine, and accountability are settled. What is interesting to me is that the Presbyterian system is designed to give the laity power in the governance of both the local church and the denomination, yet in practice it is often a clergy-dominated culture.

As I said earlier, some pastors dislike living within a governing system, even that of their own congregations. But there is no such thing as a church without people in it. When people are gathered as a worshiping community there has to be some cooperation and coordination to get things accomplished, even to produce worship on Sunday mornings. Many pastors would love to just do Sunday mornings, and maybe prayer meetings, sermon preparation, weddings, funerals, visitation, and counseling, without also adding duties beyond their local congregations.

On the local level, pastors have the most control and are not second-guessed by peers. If they never had to go to a meeting with other churches or officials, they would not mind. Sometimes these pastors fail to develop leaders, because as soon as there are multiple leaders in a congregation, it usually means having meetings and different opinions.

We all must examine our ability to love people in the context of larger church life. Pastors can be arrogant and cut themselves off from other pastors and churches, as if God wants us to lord over our flocks but not humble ourselves to listen to anyone else.

My challenge to pastors is to know the system they happen to be in. If you are in a denomination, it is short-sighted in terms of your own future and decidedly unhelpful to your congregation, if you don't know how to be a denominational player. It is especially egregious for a pastor to convey to his congregation's leadership the attitude that they need make no investment in attending regional or national meetings.

Some pastors give their elders or local leadership no motivation or incentive to get involved in or stay informed about larger church issues. Some pastors transfer their own feelings of boredom with or disdain for denominational business to those they are supposed to be training. Then when some heresy grips the church, an administrative decision must be made, or a church discipline issue arises, no one in the church knows how to deal with it in the courts of the church. Better to engage and train leaders from the beginning.

Church discipline can be easily misunderstood, but when appropriately administered is an important and positive aspect of being the church. It is necessary for the preservation of the glory of Christ, the purity of the church, and the reclamation of sinners. Yet so many elders and pastors spend very little time learning the biblical rules of discipline or the nuances of what is written about it in the Book of Church Order (if they have such a guide). Too often they wait until the last minute to know what the options are for themselves or a beloved member caught in sin.

I have seen pastors try to circumvent the rules of church discipline. They often claim to be more compassionate. I have been in presbytery meetings where the rules were ignored as we jumped to some conclusion to get rid of a scandal. In that moment I have stood and said, "Don't do this. Don't neglect the steps of discipline. It will come back to bite you." Sure enough, at least in one specific case, it did come back to bite us as a presbytery.

Let me give one little piece of advice: Follow the rules! Go by the book slowly, prayerfully, lovingly, fairly for all parties, and without being thwarted by the inconvenience and time of each particular step. None of us can do it well unless we put in the time to study how to do it. If we do this, it usually means things get done correctly without increasing the damage. There is no dealing with sin without someone being damaged. Evil and wickedness wreak havoc. They bring damage to people, ourselves, and the people we love. If we deal with it honestly, openly, with faith, with humility, and by following the rules we have agreed on (and taken vows to obey), then we will have a much better chance of restoring relationships later. If the rules are wrong, unbiblical, or more complicated than they ought to be, then change them as your church government allows.

There are politics in every church or denomination. I don't necessarily see this as a pejorative word. If we mean being manipulative, using flattery, or bribing others by opportunity or favoritism so we get our will accomplished, then we are indeed describing sinful behavior. But if we mean loving people, listening to them, pursuing relationships so we know who they are and they know us, then there is nothing wrong with it.

I confess that I have been at denominational meetings where I was astounded by how thoroughly versed some of my colleagues were in the Rules of General Assembly Operations and the Book of Church Order. I admire their knowledge and preparation so long as its intent is to strive for the peace and purity of the church and not the opposite. Their preparation challenges me to come to these meetings more prepared than I might have otherwise.

Some pastors hate confrontation, especially if they are likely to lose, so they first attempt to ascertain the winning side and then get on it. Other pastors and church leaders seem to love intellectual or political battles. They seek conflict for whatever personal agenda they might have. I am amazed at how ready some are to split a church or denomination, to slander others, or to break fellowship over fairly trivial matters. They take sides and anticipate, even encourage, people leaving.

In an age of social media, where vicious personal attacks can be made with little recourse, some pastors and Christians have seriously compromised their own holiness and testimony. They have brought disdain for and compromise to their integrity by engaging in self-righteous diatribes against particular individuals or groups. Some people need to stay off social media because it brings out the worst in them. As I have told my own congregation in regard to the use of social media, "God needs to break some of your fingers."

I took a vow when I was ordained, to be subject to my brethren. This is not always easy, especially if in conscience I think my view is correct even though it disagrees with the majority. I confess that at times I have seen some faults with my denomination and with a few of the pastors in it. But I am one with them; they are my brothers. I love them enough not to abandon them, and I hope I love them enough to call them to account if they are violating the Word of God. It is my hope that they would have the same commitment to me.

SUBMISSION

One of the things about being a Presbyterian pastor is that we commit to "being subject to our brethren." I was the pastor, but one among many elders. I didn't even vote in a meeting unless I had to break a tie. So how can one be an effective leader if everything has to be done by committee? The working out of this kind of leadership has been the cause for some difficulty in Presbyterian churches. It helps to get the leadership, submission, support, management, and unity pieces aligned.

I grew up under an independent leader. He started the church and led many of the people in it to Christ. He had personally discipled most of the people in the Word of God and taught them how to be the church. Pastor Grover Willcox was truly a great man, though like all men he had his faults. Though he was much better at certain tasks in being a pastor than I was ever able to replicate, he was still "insufficient." He could be fairly manipulative. He sometimes used guilt to coerce people into doing what he wished, and in this I feel he was spiritually abusive. Some of my peers left the church and abandoned their faith as a result of his behavior. When

I became a pastor, I wanted to emulate the good and repudiate the bad that I saw in his leadership.

He was strong-minded and of strong opinions. I needed to establish some spiritual independence from him for my own mental and spiritual health, which I did during my teen years. I was in the youth group, the Conqueror's Club. It was a wonderful, dynamic, and growing youth ministry. Our pastor believed in developing leadership in young people and used training and participation in evangelism to help achieve it.

At one club meeting he announced that he and his wife, after prayer, had decided this particular year to not have club members nominate club officers. Instead, he and his wife had chosen whom to nominate and at the beginning of the next school year we would get the chance to vote on those they had chosen. He announced my name as someone he felt the Holy Spirit had led him to nominate for secretary of the club. This caused an immediate negative reaction within me, as if someone were taking away my right to make my own decisions about who to nominate or to stand for an office.

I told Pastor I didn't feel led to take this office, and he told me to pray over it and wait until the elections. Some months later the election came, and he called for a vote on his nominations. I raised my hand and withdrew my nomination. Then the young man he had nominated for president also asked to withdraw his nomination. At this point Pastor stopped the meeting, and he told the other young man and me that he wanted our mothers to accompany us to meet with him privately at his home later that week. I dutifully told my mother and added that I resented someone making choices for me. She agreed to come.

When we had the meeting at Pastor's house, he began by pointing out that both the boy nominated for president and I were in homes of single parent mothers. This was obviously true. Then he warned us that we were both in danger of becoming homosexuals if we didn't learn how to discipline ourselves and follow God's will. This was so out of left field for me that I could neither understand its relevance nor its utter nonsense. I did, however, become absolutely convinced that this was not coming from the Holy Spirit and was nothing but coercion.

The other boy's mother looked at him, and she told him she thought he should take the position, and he then agreed. My mom looked at me and asked, "What do you want to do?" I said "No." She then looked at Pastor and said, "You have your answer." I am so proud of my mother for that day.

In this particular case my pastor showed his insufficiency, as I too have unfortunately shown mine at times.

Presbyterianism attracted me due to its system of accountability with elders and the presbytery, the group of elders and pastors in a region that get together for decisions. I believe every pastor needs such accountability. I know I have an intense, strong personality. Sometimes people have told me they felt intimidated by me. I knew I wasn't doing anything on purpose to make them afraid. I don't think anyone was physically afraid of me. Yet they felt intimidated. I have consciously always sought to be open about my agenda, but even that can bother people who want a pastor who is softer and has less certainty. I grew up in Newark and don't always know how to beat around the bush. This can be off-putting for some people.

So I need, want, and value accountability. I want to be reined in when I am wrong because I know I can be wrong. I became a Presbyterian and have since always had to work with and under elders and the presbytery. Yet I think I am a strong leader. We (the church session and I) had to figure out how to work together. I was blessed to be given a great deal of trust by my elders (our church leadership system includes unpaid leaders called elders). I invited their opinions about the worship and preaching, and I was blessed that they never sought to micromanage or take over those weekly decisions.

I always sought their counsel about the structure of the ministry and the hiring and firing of staff, but we agreed that they would not attempt to manage the staff or step in and interfere with my decisions. They had every right to evaluate my decision-making and even to take away authority from me if they wished. I might have had to resign if I objected to that, but thankfully that kind of a confrontation never happened.

There were a time or two when I had to ask, "Do you want to manage the staff and have me step back from that?" I think the reality of this frightened them a bit, as it should. Management by committee is not a good style of leadership in any organization. I don't think it is wise for elders to take it on themselves to rebuke or criticize a staff member based on their own opinion, unless it is egregious behavior. I think it is tempting for elders to do that if they suddenly or impulsively realize they don't like something, such as a song or the style of music. That conversation needs to go through the pastor or executive pastor so that staff members don't feel they have more than one supervisor or boss. Obviously if an elder sees something as sinful or harmful to the body, he should certainly speak into the situation.

One of my biggest lessons in submission came by way of a conflict between my commitment to the US Army as a chaplain and my role as a pastor. One day my wife Joan and I were driving to an outdoor nature center to get some exercise. We were listening to the radio when suddenly the news broke in to say that Saddam Hussein and the Iraqi army had invaded the nation of Kuwait. I turned to Joan and said, "This means we will go to war." I knew that the US could not stand by and let this go unchallenged.

As I thought about it, I knew chaplains would be needed. I was a member of a Reserve Combat Support Hospital, and I wasn't sure whether the unit would be specified. So I called a higher ranking friend in the chaplaincy and asked if he would put my name on the volunteer list to be called up. He asked, "Are you sure, because you will be first in line."

That very night we had a session meeting at church. I informed the session of my action. They questioned me about whether this was an individual decision or one forced on me by the Army. I told them it was my decision. They immediately made a motion to have my name removed from the volunteer list and unanimously voted to have me do so. Mr. Schmidt, as the oldest elder said, "If you are called up by your unit we will support you, but you have no right to make this decision on your own and leave your responsibilities here."

This happened pretty fast, and I was stunned. I admitted to them that they had the right to make that decision, but that I felt God had called me to be in the Army, to minister to soldiers, and if we were going to war, I needed to help. So I told them I would pray over it and let them know what I would do. I realized that if I could not submit to their decision, I would have to resign as pastor from a church I had helped to start, a ministry I loved, and from a group of people who had loved me well.

It was a hard week. My pride was hurt, I didn't think my motives were wrong, and I was embarrassed to think I'd have to call my friend at headquarters and back out. No one spoke to me about my decision that week, but later Joan told me the elders were calling her throughout the week asking what I was thinking and which way I was leaning. I finally came to the realization that the elders were indeed correct. I had taken vows to pastor this church and had no right to make such a unilateral decision. So I called my friend and asked him to remove me from the list. I told the elders and ate some humble pie.

Within a few months my unit was indeed mobilized, and I went with them to Desert Storm and served the soldiers and patients in my hospital in Saudi Arabia, Iraq, and Kuwait. The night before I left, I told Joan I felt I had been prepared for this ministry all my life, and she told me, "Then it is right that you go." My ministry there and the struggles I had are subjects for a different story, but my church supported me completely. One of the greatest emotional moments in my life was to arrive at the airport in Chattanooga upon my return from war and find a hundred people waiting for me, along with my family, singing the doxology and feel their affection, loyalty, and pride.

But there were a few people who weren't happy at my return. It wasn't that they wished I had died in the war, but they did hope my absence would allow and opportunity for them to choose another pastor.

The parties in the congregation who saw my absence as a good thing decided to leave the church within a year of my return. This departure included a few church officers. Some of it was due to the comparison they made with the really good pastoring they received while I was gone (for which I was thankful). Some of it was due to the frustration they had with the cross-cultural vision of the church, which they knew I would not surrender. And some was due to conflict with me personally.

[On a side note: I think it is despicable for churches that have pastors who also serve as Reserve Chaplains to fire them when they are mobilized. Obviously if the pastor must be gone for too long, or for too many deployments, it is wises for the church to have a stable, resident pastor. But this should be worked out prior to such deployments, through written agreement, so there is honesty and understanding between both parties. I eventually retired from the Army during Iraqi Freedom rather than take a fourth deployment because I knew it would hurt the church.]

DISCIPLINE AND RESTORATION IN LEADERSHIP

I want to include some words about submission with regard to being disciplined by a church court and hopefully restored. I have had the unfortunate experience of seeing some pastors in the denomination go through discipline in their presbyteries. It was unfortunate because sin is unfortunate, but it was not always unfortunate with regard to the outcome.

The outcome of discipline by and from a presbytery or church council depends on several factors. One crucial factor is the attitude of the person who has sinned. Is he truly repentant? Is he humble enough to receive and profit from the discipline? Is he entrusting himself to Christ, or is he maneuvering and trying to protect himself from punishment? One way you can tell if a man is humble and trusting Christ is his willingness to tell the truth and accept whatever comes from the hands of his brothers. This can be extremely hard, scary, and risky for a pastor who has sinned. Not every presbytery knows how to restore sinners, and not every presbytery is willing to make the effort.

Sometimes pastors who fall into sin are more worried about keeping their jobs than they are with breaking cleanly from their sin. These men don't want to own up to their sins or take the risk of public rebuke and embarrassment. Proverbs 18:3 says that *"with shame comes disgrace."* The moment of facing our shame publicly is traumatic, and how a person handles it gives testimony to repentance and faith. Sometimes pastors choose to leave the denomination and start their own independent congregation rather than go through the discipline process.

As I have intimated, another factor is the presbytery. I wish our Book of Church Order had more in it about restoration, but our denomination has purposefully left this to the subjective judgment of each presbytery. Not all elders or presbyteries agree with how to deal with fallen brothers. Some pastors think once a man has confessed to adultery that he should never serve again as a pastor, so for them restoration to the pastorate is not something they are willing to consider. Other presbyteries have worked hard to bring brothers back, either from sexual sins, addictions, or other kinds of sinful behavior.

For those of us in the ministry, we should fear God more than anything else and that includes our loss of status or our paychecks. If you are called and you fall but then repent, it is honorable for you to seek to be restored. If your presbytery refuses to help you, then they are accountable before God for their hardness of heart, if that be the case. My advice is to submit to their direction, even if it is humiliating and hard. As you provide evidence of true repentance and a humble trust in God by your willingness to go to counseling or engage in guided restoration, then the presbytery may have evidence that God's grace is at work in your life. Trust is easy to lose and hard to gain back, but in the Lord's mercy it is possible.

LEADERSHIP TRANSITION

I wish to speak here of transition, either by way of being called to another congregation or ministry, being fired, or retiring. Is there some way pastors can shepherd their flocks to prepare them for change?

Sooner or later the pastor is going to leave. He will be sent out, walk out, kicked out, retire, or be carried out. My experience is that very few pastors talk about this reality. Some pastors have refused to prepare for it and then die, leaving their congregations in crisis that lasts for years.

I always thought it would be helpful for church members to know how to get rid of me if they didn't like me, so we could all avoid the games people play when they want to get a new pastor. To that end, I explained in the New Members class how to bring a complaint directly to the pastor. If that's not satisfactory, then they should know how to involve other elders, and then how to bring a complaint to the session. I taught against gossip and political manipulation, and I called for honest confrontation.

I tried to have evaluations of my performance by the congregation once every five years. Some of my elders didn't like this practice and were afraid it would create division. Thankfully that was never the case, though at times it did expose some dissatisfaction. I think giving the membership a chance to speak about their concerns about my performance helped to kill a lot of potential grumbling.

I am aware that some pastors last only three to five years in a church. One of the patterns I have seen is for a pastor to get into conflict, and after it is over decide he is "called" by God to another place of ministry. I have heard that many pastors leave a call within two years of a building program, an experience that's always rife with conflict. If a pastor can't stay in a church after he finds out that not everyone absolutely loves him (usually by the third year), he probably won't get to the place where he can lead the church to the next level of ministry and potential.

Some congregations might be accused of being sneaky when they call a new pastor. I have a prejudice that if a pastor is looking for a new call, but he won't tell his current session about his desire, then there is something wrong with the way that relationship has been handled. Why would the next church think he will treat them differently? I think it is good for sessions to ask their pastors for some kind of game plan or agreed-upon rules for how such an experience should be played out if it should ever happen.

Will the present pastor train his congregation how to conduct a search for the new pastor? Most don't, since they usually leave before such a committee is formed. I had the opportunity to retire from my pulpit though not from ministry, and we took almost five years together as pastor and congregation to get ready for it. As part of that transition, I preached for months on what we need in a pastor, and how a congregation should treat him. I then trained the search committee, but I refused to be part of it so that whoever they recommended to the congregation would be their fault (for good or ill) and not mine.

I have the honor of continuing to worship in the congregation in which I pastored when I am home. I realize that my continued presence could be viewed as a threat by the new pastor and his wife, but they have treated Joan and me with great honor, love, and courtesy. That is to their credit. Also, to God's credit, he has helped me (for the most part) to keep my mouth shut. If I ever have any criticisms, I keep them to myself and pray for and advocate for the success of our new pastor.

This goes against every bit of practical advice I received in seminary and in the denomination. The advice that our new pastor was given was much as I had heard for years. Men were and are told, "If you follow a pastor with a long tenure, make sure you aren't the first one there as you will inevitably be a sacrificial lamb. Let someone else fill the gap for two years. Let him get fired and then apply." We don't believe this has to be the case, but anyone should see the worldly wisdom in it.

I want to challenge pastors to prepare their flocks for pastoral transition and not simply leave them behind to figure out things for themselves. To do so is not leadership, and a sign that ministry is more about yourself rather than the church over which God has made you an overseer.

SUGGESTIONS

1. One aspect of leadership is being able to cast vision for specific aspects of the ministry of the church. Does the pastor have a vision for how his elders or leadership group should function and what they are supposed to achieve? If a pastor has no concept of how to build a leadership team or what the leadership should cohesively and in a unified way accomplish, he will create a leadership vacuum where negative and reactionary ideas may fill the space.

2. Does the pastor have a vision for mercy ministry? Does he have a vision for how the deacons or mercy team should function and what they should be trying to accomplish? He must not only have a solid theology of mercy but also know how to minister mercy in a way that truly helps the poor and suffering as well as mobilizes and blesses the church.

3. If a leader is ignorant in an area of ministry needed by the congregation, he needs to seek training. And training does not mean simply reading a book or

listening to a seminar and then doing nothing different. A leader must learn and then do.

4. The pastor is the trainer of trainers and needs to recruit gifted practitioners and build systems that accomplish the vision he has cast for the church. Then he needs to keep recruiting, training, and deploying people who can take responsibility when positions need to be filled.

PART SEVEN
CULTURAL AWARENESS
SERVING AS AN AMBASSADOR OF THE GOSPEL

*I see that in every way you are very religious. For as I walked
around and looked carefully at your objects of worship, I even
saw an altar with this inscription: to an unknown God.*
Acts 17:22–23

If you haven't felt insufficient, then this area will surely leave you
panting for oxygen. I hope you can boast in your weakness in the
humility (if not humiliation) it brings, so you can call on God for
wisdom and help. Compentance in understanding ethnic culture
and peace play a strong part in our view of ourselves and others.
this cultural competence—or lack of it—colors our view of theology
and the practice of our faith, worship, and ethical behavior.

Culture is powerful over our lives in more ways than we realize.
I speak here of the patterns of life that direct and control us in our
social behaviors and attitudes. Much of this happens without our
conscious thought. Whenever social behaviors are violated, it can
be jarring, unnerving, distressing, and even infuriating. We typically feel comfortable when life moves along the path of our
cultural expectations and may fail to realize (due to our ignorance

of the culture of others) that other people may be in emotional distress and increasingly annoyed with us when we act out of the norm of their cultural context.

I am not speaking here about the philosophical basis of culture, although it would be hard to ignore it completely. Scholars and intellectuals speak about culture and how it lays the foundation for a society's worldview (how it thinks and makes cultural decisions), both in the area of ethics and ontology. The late Dr. Francis Schaeffer used this philosophical approach as a means of discerning why Western culture was declining, especially in its commitment to Christian values. He often referred to the historic direction of culture as a post-Christian era. There are tremendous insights to be gained from understanding how universities, the arts, media, and various political movements have been shaped by philosophers and their ideas and why society seems headed in certain directions.

Studying the philosophy behind watershed movements is a bit like looking backstage at history. There are various aha moments when it suddenly becomes clear that events and leaders didn't drop out of the sky when history turned a corner. There are ideas and reasons behind the motivations and passions of history and culture makers. However, such a focus on philosophy without an attendant appreciation of ethnic and socioeconomic variation can often leave us making statements that are incomplete in their analysis and might actually only fit one ethnic group, race, or class level.

What one preacher might look at in history as an absolutely wonderful era might have been disastrous for another ethnic group which suffered during that period. So it has been with Black folk. I remember Dr. John Perkins saying once at the annual conference of the Christian Community Development Association, referring to the evangelical call to go back to the culture and standards of our God-fearing American founders and forefathers. He said, "I don't want to go back there; I would've been a slave."

Another way some think of culture is as a process of education and civilization. Those "people of culture" seem to know how to appreciate the finer things of life as they define them. They are usually literate, know how to engage in intelligent conversation, and have a common commitment to defining what is excellent according to their standards. These are the people who enjoy opera, classical music, fine novels, great poetry, ballet, sculpture, and paintings. Their tastes are refined, so they say, and they know how and when to take their tea and what utensils to use when at a state dinner. They have a specific kind of vocabulary and are adept at syntax. They usually are well-traveled and well-connected. A good many of them have a working knowledge of intellectual history.

I am *not* speaking of "high culture" versus "low culture." There are members of all ethnic groups, and within ethnic groups, who have varying levels of education and varying levels of an educated palate. However, there are those who assume that "high culture" is innately European and that all people should be lifted into an appreciation of a Western standard of civilization. To not do so is to be considered inferior in cultural taste or simply uncultured. Arrogance and snobbery have never been cultural incentives for me.

I specifically want to speak of competency in understanding how ethnic culture and race play a strong part in our view of ourselves and others. I want to speak of how that competency—or lack of it—colors our view of theology and the practice of our Christian religion, worship, and ethical behavior.

An area of culture that escapes many pastors' understanding is that of wealth and poverty. Most people notice wealth and poverty, but not the culture that is built around them and how those cultures affect, and even control, the people in them. Most American pastors are middle-class, if not by economic background then at least by education. Some pastors have grown up in poverty and have done all they could to escape it, but not to engage it. Some pastors would like to be wealthy and minister to the rich. Certainly rich people need Jesus too, yet understanding the culture of wealth is different than just wanting to be rich.

Dealing with poverty and its culture is a spiritual issue and not simply a circumstantial one. According to the Bible, we dare not despise the poor, and we must preach the Gospel to them, so this then is a matter of Christian obedience. Unfortunately, many middle-class pastors appear to think they have the choice to avoid ministry to the poor. As I read the Gospels, I cannot come to that conclusion. I have written a great deal on this subject on my blog and in my book, *Merciful*. I encourage you to read those to discover more ideas and methods on this topic.[1]

Some churches have "transformation" in their vision or mission statements almost as a motto: We will transform the city. Some Christians don't think transformation is possible until Jesus comes back and think it is presumptuous of any church to speak of it. But Christians are in fact told to *"make disciples of all nations."* Does that mean people from all nations or the nations themselves? Can righteousness ever be achieved by a nation? If righteousness is what exalts a nation and sin is a reproach to any people, do we have any hope before Jesus comes that such a nation could exist?

Is it only about Israel when the Scripture says, *"Blessed is the nation whose God is the Lord"*? (Ps. 33:12). Could it ever be said about any other ethnic group? Is national transformation possible only by individual conversions, or would it take some greater amount of moral and political reformation? Does a nation have to be totally transformed to be righteous or is it always going to be mixed with sin? Is there really any such thing as "revival" or "reformation"?

Believers push for legislation to change laws about abortion, homosexuality, and divorce. We have had movements for temperance, the abolition of slavery, the creation of civil rights. We have men and women who go into politics to be "Christian" in government and try to bring about moral and ethical change on a national scale. Even pastors who demand the church stay out of such things might applaud Christian individuals who give themselves to those efforts.

Some churches have been instrumental in spiritual and cultural transformation in neighborhoods, cities, and nations, while some churches have completely lost their Gospel message to pursue social reformation. On the other hand, some churches have lost their Gospel credibility by being silent in the face of great injustice, racism, and evil. Yet, I think history shows that Christianity, through the evangelizing of people, the planting of churches, and the discipling of believers, has a social and community conscience that often has changed cultures for the better.

Transformation is best thought of as local and temporal. Final and definitive transformation only happens with the cataclysmic return of Jesus Christ. The saying "All politics is local" is true. To forget that "on-the-block" importance hurts both politicians and pastors. That is why the local church, especially in its immediate neighborhood as the biblical "city on a hill," is able to effectively do good works among the lost. Being *"the light of the world"* (Matt. 5:14) is I believe a corporate image, not simply an individual one.

Doing good works so the lost can see them are not good works done within the four walls of the church. They must be done in the broader world, and in specific communities.

Christian social transformation is usually temporary. Historically, evil has overtaken cultures and societies even after times of reformation and revival. I believe there will be no eternal or permanent transformation until the final appearance of Jesus and the creation of the new heavens and new earth. Nevertheless, Gospel change and truth have historically brought cultures to greater times of goodness, justice, and peace. Gospel conversion, acts of mercy, justice, and righteousness have eternal effects for the individuals, families, tribes, and nations that have come to Christ.

Transformation is not to be sought with hubris or presumption, but in humble application of Gospel love, truth, and service by churches, through the power of God's grace, in neighborhoods where they exist. Transformation is sought against the evils that oppress people, even as believers seek to break the yokes of injustice. In all of this, we must be faithful in calling people to the cross and to belief in Christ. Isaiah 58:6 says, *"Is not this the kind of fasting I have chosen: to loose the chains of injustice and untie the cords of the yoke, to set the oppressed free and break every yoke?"*

Unfortunately, too many churches take no notice of their own neighborhoods or communities; they serve only themselves. They give an apologetic for their existence as only meaningful for believers and wonder why they have such few visitors. Pastors must lead with a balanced vision of what they are to do personally and what it is possible for their congregations to do. Pastors need wisdom as to what their presbytery and denomination might do for their regions and general culture. Pastors should give encouragement and guidance as to what individual members might do in their vocations and for their neighbors. Each level of the church has a part to play in impacting the world for God's glory.

COMMUNITY ENGAGEMENT

Also, seek the peace and prosperity of the city
to which I have carried you into exile. Pray to the
Lord for it, because if it prospers, you too will prosper.
Jeremiah 29:7

Some pastors are great at this, some are terrible, and some are confused and conflicted. There are pastors who don't see any reason for community engagement, as they believe their task is in the local church which, as their employer, has called them to preach, teach, counsel, and comfort. Some pastors have spent their entire ministries treating everything outside of the church walls as "the world," or as a distraction.

My desire here is not to engage the Two Kingdoms debate but rather to speak about several community engagement issues. One is the reality that our charge as pastors means that we often must represent our organization, the local church, to outside agencies and to the broader community.

We live in a politicized atmosphere in the United States. Some in the conservative community feel that the world is threatening to our children and our Christian way of life. Do you as the pastor seek to protect your flock from a dangerous world, to ignore the world, or to invade the world so you can help change it? Sometimes the outside community suspects that Christians don't care about anything but ourselves. They don't see us as a friend or helpful to the community, but as a closed-off institution. Are you as a pastor able to build bridges to the broader community that often holds negative views of the church and Christians?

How much time should a pastor devote to interacting with community leaders, institutions, and organizations as a representative of the church? How much time should a pastor give to meet with pastor fellowships or clergy organizations? How much time should a pastor give for personal involvement in schools, nonprofits, or civic efforts? How collaborative can the church afford to be with community efforts?

The answer to this is going to depend on things such as the willingness of the church and its leadership to share their pastor with other institutions. Some will depend on what the pastor chooses to do or feels comfortable doing. Some will depend on the cultural and contextual issues of his ministry. Some will depend on whether the pastor is able to politically navigate the larger world of the neighborhood, town, or city without losing sight of his main calling.

As a pastor, I have to remember I am always a Christian, and I always represent my church even if I mistakenly think that what I do on my own time is my business. I also have to remember that the more time I give to other activities, the less time I have to care for the people and ministries of my church. There are so many good things I could do, and sometimes I am asked to do them by the world outside the church. Almost any civic or community effort is hungry for volunteers and will happily take any hours you can give.

You should think through the reasons for any such involvements. What is your goal in working in and with the community? What do you hope to accomplish with your volunteer service or involvement? Are you becoming engaged with community affairs because you think you can make a difference and see it as part of your ministry and love to the community? How will it help the church and enhance its reputation? Will anyone start coming to the church because of what you do? Will it bring any resources to the church? Will your connections to various community institutions protect or bless the people of your congregation?

Community engagement is not simply about pastoral involvement, it is also about church mobilization for community impact. Pastors who motivate, inspire, encourage, train, and deploy their members into significant and impactful ministry within the community influence far beyond their personal investment of time. The pastor's relationships with community leaders is important, but what really makes a difference is if the lay people of the congregation are engaged with elevating community assets, remedying community ailments, and standing with the community on issues of justice.

It is in the labor of love within the community by the church body that church members get to share a witness for Jesus, both in word and deed. Our acts of love, mercy, sacrifice, and kindness within the neighborhood give us credibility, grounds for having conversations, and opportunities to meet people. Pastors need to think strategically with church leadership about where and when and how to launch members into service, and they always need to think about sharing the message of the Gospel tied to their good works. Dispersing your members all over the city to volunteer for nonprofits will give them a taste of service but usually won't translate into them bringing neighborhood folks into the church.

Pastors must beware of engaging in community outreach to stroke their own egos. It feels nice to be thanked, admired, and applauded. Flattery, status, and esteem are powerful perfumes.

The care of the church is usually an all-consuming commitments for pastors. Being on call for all kinds of emergencies makes the pastor a little "iffy" for regular meetings. Watch out for the temptation to serve on every board that invites you. Even service on presbytery and denominational agencies and boards, to which you have some obligation, must be carefully evaluated. Excessive outside service will rob your congregation of you.

Your work in your own local church defines your reputation as a pastor. If you don't feel loved enough, the solution is not more scattered commitments but some real Holy Ghost Gospel work in your heart and possibly an honest discussion with church leaders. Many congregations do a terrible job of loving on their pastors; many give meager and sparing encouragement. They seem to worry about praising him too much or paying him too much because they don't want him to get a big head.

Sometimes you must give of yourself, either for the connection of your congregation to the community or for the sake of the Kingdom. Far too often, boards and other committees not specifically helping the ministries of the church are time thieves, and pastors (usually) make lousy board members anyway. We are used to speaking with authority. Other board members don't always bow to our opinions as they see themselves as an "equal" board member (imagine that). Once on a board, we don't usually like taking on additional assignments, as board membership leads to more involvement in the organization it directs.

Yet some pastors do nothing in the broader community. They do nothing in their presbyteries or denominations either. For them it is the local church and (hopefully) their family. Sometimes the pastor, if he is to be effective in ministry to the community, must give his time and energy to make and develop broader neighborhood and community connections.

In poor and depressed communities, churches are sometimes the only advocate for the people there. What affects the community affects the members of the church, so the pastor can't afford to simply be the shepherd of his flock. He must also be a spokesman, a protector, a chaplain, a parish priest, and even an organizer. My suspicion is that the comfort of being a middle-class pastor too often allows one to develop a theology of non-community involvement.

The needs of the community and the congregation will never be totally synonymous. The community is made up of believers and unbelievers, even those who oppose the Gospel, and members of various sects and religions with which we don't agree. Here the pastor has to be wise as to when and with whom he can be allied to stand against evil and injustice, and with whom he can align to pursue solutions of mercy and peace. Sometimes these alliances can only be temporary and issue-based. Pastors and Christians don't have to abandon their testimony or faith to work with others; in fact, it is a great opportunity and place to be a witness for Christ.

I pastored an intentionally cross-cultural church. I was concerned that African Americans not be put in a position of abandoning their cultural and ethnic community as they joined with White people and others to worship. Often Black members of our church were accused by family and friends of being disloyal to the Black community for being part of our church. Solidarity is a very important value in the Black community, especially in opposition to historic White racism. To help my African American members stay connected to the Black community I knew I had to be connected to Black pastors in the city.

Then one summer a Covenant Seminary student, who happened to be from South Africa, came to our city and pastored at the mission that would become New City. His name was Neville Jacobs. Pastor Jacobs was designated "colored" in apartheid South Africa. While in Chattanooga, he reached out to several Black pastors and was invited to join the Black Ministers Union. I eventually was invited to visit too. The group met every Tuesday morning at one of the Black churches in town, and I was formally part of it for more than twenty-five years. The name later changed to the Clergy Koinonia. These men, and later some women, were very gracious to me. Of course, at first, some of them didn't trust me at all. Some found out I was a "conservative" and assumed that all of my social views were consistent with the conservative Evangelicals they knew. Some of their own members were Evangelical, but that term was not one used very often in African American religious circles.

When they found out my wife was Black, it put me in a different category, but I was still suspect. What really helped me was to humble myself and learn from the older men there. They taught me so many things about being a pastor, about church, even how to dress like a preacher in the Black community. From then on I always wore a tie and jacket when I preached. As the years went by, several of them were invited to preach in my church and I was invited to preach in theirs as well as at revivals. The simple fact of being invited to preach at a Black church gave me immediate and positive identification in the broader Black community.

This was a definite time commitment. We met every Tuesday morning for about two hours, and that was if I didn't go to lunch with some of them after the meeting. While some of the leaders of the group were men of God and very good preachers, some didn't believe the whole Bible. I knew that a few of them had terrible reputations morally and some were not trusted even by Black folk. Navigating the relationships was not always easy.

There were times when they asked me to stand with them about various social or community issues. Most of the time I agreed with their positions, but not always. Sometimes my connections to financial resources were able to help them as a group or as individuals. I hold it as a great honor to have been included by them.

The relationship I had with these men became a foundation for other things in the community. For a while I was a member of the NAACP. The mayor asked me to serve on the city's Human Rights Commission and then to be on a committee to help choose a new chief of police. The new chief asked me to attend the Civilian Police Academy, which I did.

Inner-city communities need advocates before city government and the police force. If you don't develop those relationships (both with people in the 'hood and with authorities) on a positive basis prior to some horrible act of injustice or misunderstanding, it is much harder to play catch-up when everyone is angry or defensive.

The elders of my church knew of my involvements and generally supported and affirmed them. I felt it was essential to give our congregation credibility in the Black community, and I think that was by and large achieved through these pastoral relationships. But there were always those Black pastors who could not conceive of a mentally healthy Black person worshiping with White folk.

I encourage all pastors who work in minority communities, whether they are themselves a member of it or not, to reach out to the established churches and pastors that are already present. I think it is a great insult to come into a community and not pay respect to those who have served and paid their dues of ministry and life in that neighborhood. Black pastors want to be treated as peers and equals to White pastors and understandably don't respond well to having a lay person attempt to be the connecting point between congregations.

Some indigenous pastors will not welcome you, some will see you as competition, and some will actively seek to make your ministry difficult. But seek those who have been praying for years for reinforcements and help. If we enter a neighborhood acting as if we are the Messiah, we insult others and dishonor Christ. There is only one Messiah, and his name is Jesus! We do not seek to plant new churches as a way of declaring that everyone else has failed, but only to win more people to Christ.

It is silly to assume that everyone in a neighborhood is owned by any one particular church. Most mature pastors know this is true, but it is hard for them not to be resentful and envious when a new church plant arrives, made up mostly of White middle-class folks who seem to have all the resources and don't act like good neighbors; especially if they spread a lot of hype about how they are now going to "change the city."

We don't have to make things harder than they are by refusing to humble ourselves. We show humility by going to leaders already present and introducing ourselves, asking them for advice and guidance, and being willing to share ourselves and our resources with them. Some folks won't work with you, some will actively oppose you, some will tolerate you, and yet others will become great friends.

Reformed Black pastors need to build bridges to other Black pastors as well and not assume they will be automatically welcomed in a neighborhood. Sometimes there is a very specific rejection by the clerical Black establishment of Black men from a predominantly White denomination, or who include White members in their church. This is usually overcome once friendships are formed and community people realize the new Black Reformed pastor is not rejecting the Black community, or Black culture, or his own identity.

I strongly encourage every Black Reformed pastor to have a radio show on a station that is listened to by the Black community. To have a strong biblical voice on such stations will gain them name recognition in the Black community and attract folks to their church.

RACIAL AND ETHNIC COMPONENTS
OF CULTURE

For Jews do not associate with Samaritans.
John 4:9

I have a pair of glasses that help my eyes see things far away and things very close. I can read signs at a distance and small print right in front of me. Not only that, but they are sensitive to light. So when I am outside, my lenses darken, and when I walk inside the lenses becomes lighter.

Sometimes I forget I am wearing these glasses. If the sky becomes dark while I am driving, it looks darker than it is because of my lenses. Perspective through a lens is a way to understand our natural biases and prejudices when it comes to ethnic or racial culture. I use the term without censure because some of our biases and prejudices are not necessarily negative. But we tend to define things according to the cultural education and experiences we have had.

By "cultural education" I don't mean a course we took in school to make us think and act like the cultural animals we are. Most of this education is what we might call imprinting. It was modeled for us, we learned to understand and explain reality in a certain way, and we may or may not have attempted to analyze it intellectually. Culture is an intricately woven part of our lives, yet is mostly autonomic; it doesn't require thinking on our part. What side of the road do you drive on, or what side of the sidewalk do you walk on? How do you dress, and how do you judge the dress of others? How do you eat your food, and why do you use utensils? Do you cover your mouth when you yawn, cough, or sneeze? Do you open doors for women, the elderly, or small children? Do you feel sentimental when you see a puppy, or do you feel hungry?

How do you deal with time and keeping appointments? Do you become angry when someone arrives late, or do you become angry because your friend leaves in the middle of an emotional moment because of an appointment? Are you fatalistic in what happens to you and refuse to accept personal responsibility, or are you blame-driven and think it must always be someone's fault? How do you see and feel about authority and rules? How thoroughly do you clean your sinks, floors, walls, and furniture? How do you feel about eating everything on your plate or seeing others waste their food?

I have found that most people in America don't analyze things holistically. Some pastors seek to define things purely from a theological framework. Others analyze things only ideologically or politically. Still others judge things almost exclusively from a racial or ethnic grid. These limitations in analysis are not only naïve, but sometimes embarrassing and occasionally dangerous. We tend to give each component either too little attention or too much.

When it comes to theology, some tend to think that it can be received in a vacuum and that our present way of thinking and living has no effect on it whatsoever. I remember when books on "Black Theology" came out, and professors and pastors I knew scoffed and said no such thing could exist. In their minds, there was only Theology, with a capital "T." Later I realized that on their shelves were books titled *Scottish Theology*. How could they not connect the two? It is good to admit one's ignorance (insufficiency) in order to become a better learner. As long as we insist we know and understand everything, then much will escape us. Part of cultural ignorance is making assumptions based on limited information.

One day a young African American student at a local Christian college told me about a conversation she had with a White student who had grown up on the mission field, a person known as a third culture kid. He confidently told her that African Americans had no separate culture from White American kids; they were all just Americans to him. With that comment he casually dismissed much of what was important to this young woman in her family, history, and church. This young man made a hasty declaration based on an incomplete analysis of what he was seeing, or failing to see. His ignorance was painful to hear, especially if one assumes that missionary kids had the tools to make a better cultural analysis.

Some of the ramifications of such ignorance come out in White reaction to things like the celebration of Black History Month. History is of course very much part of culture, and poignant moments of history affect our emotions, self-image, and view of others. When someone has no knowledge of the history of other ethnic groups, it is easy to be dismissive as to how current events could be tied to those of the past.

In the South, there remains an emotional hold on those who wave the Confederate flag regarding the "War of Northern Aggression," known in other places as the Civil War. Why do some hold onto the idea of being a rebel as a noble and good thing? Why is there nostalgic affection for what was a horrendous moment of American history (I say this as someone whose ancestors fought in the Mississippi Rifle Regiments)? Much of it has to do with a selective view of history and an almost complete denial of how that history affected others. If one believes that slavery was not such a bad thing, or that racial slavery was a "step up" for Africans, or that slave owners were benign if not compassionate, then one might think the whole war had to do with Northern tyranny that took away Southerners' private property.

Such thinking is completely irrational since these same people would likely fight to the death before they would be anyone's slave. What right did White people have in the first place to hold a human being as property, simply based on race? How can any American act as if someone else should have been patient for slavery (or segregation) to end when we, as Americans, couldn't be patient for a tax on tea to go away? It is a failure of logic, with examples going back at least as far as Aristotle, that slaves deserve to be slaves since they are slaves, and are indeed (and should be) content in that condition.

I would argue at this point that there is not simply cultural or ethnic ignorance at play but also pure and wicked racism. My ethnic and cultural background might make me see things from a jaundiced perspective, but racism is worse that that. Racists in fact may not be as ignorant as those with cultural tunnel vision. They may see the facts, but purposefully define them differently, give vicious meanings to them, and use them to justify their hate. Racism takes disparity and uses it as an excuse for more disparity.

Racism is hate, and it is murder. It is a denial of the image of God in a human being. It is an arrogance and pride, a sense of superiority about one's race or ethnicity and thus a form of idolatry. Racism is deceptive toward those on the outside and self-deceptive to those inside its sphere. It is insidious and aggressive in the way it pursues harm to those it declares inferior. Racism attempts to justify its actions through an appeal to rights and sometimes carries out acts of terror that any human being would find horrifying if done to them or theirs. I speak of such things as race-based slavery, racial breeding, lynching, economic and social segregation, foul-mouthed hostility, ethnic cleansing, and even genocidal acts such as the Holocaust.

One of the results of cultural ignorance is to assume the best about members of our own race. We might say that surely they could not have meant what they just said in a racist way or that an event could not have had a racial basis for it. Our cultural and ethnic bias often is dismissive and justifying of our ethnic representative's action and suspicious of the motive of another ethnic representative's interpretation. Thus we are surprised and shocked when racism is finally exposed; it is almost as if we cannot believe such a thing could really exist, at least not in our kind of folks.

I am amazed, confounded, and dismayed at the history of Nazi Germany. It almost defies belief that a so-called "Christian nation" could fall into such delusion about itself and other people groups. But I also am amazed when I see photos of hundreds of American White people, sometimes with children by them, watching with apparent enjoyment a Black man hanging from a tree. These historical realities must keep us focused on the fact that evil has and does exist, and if it is not resisted may come back again.

In a church world that attempts to be missional, plant churches, and build congregations with representatives from various ethnic groups, racism is a factor we must deal with. It isn't the reason behind every fear and criticism. It is not, and should not be, the go-to excuse for dismissing the questions or concerns people have about crossing ethnic, cultural, and socioeconomic lines. However, to not take its reality seriously, or to fail to realize that some people actually do harbor it, will have consequences.

ETHICAL IN AN INTER-ETHNIC WORLD

Here is the necessary tie-in between being ethically competent as a pastor and being culturally competent. If a pastor is ignorant of the ethnic and racial motives of people and how those affect their values, judgments, and behaviors, then how can he see or be aware of some of the ethical challenges presented? If one is dismissive of racial prejudice and racism, then one cannot possibly understand, stand up for, or preach about justice in a multiethnic society in any meaningful way.

Steps toward racism may begin with ignorance and then proceed to false and generalized explanation—stereotypes. In a multicultural world, one of the most foolish things we can do as pastors is to fail to see how closely held cultural and ethnic values are to people. When we attempt to explain things theologically, with no appreciation for the ethnic culture of the biblical writers or the ethnic culture of the people we are trying to reach, we are at best ineffective and at worst harmful.

As Christian leaders, we are often insufficient and sometimes willfully negligent in pursuing cultural and emotional intelligence. The intersection of culture and emotions can give us insight into why people speak, act, or feel the way they do. If we diagnose issues incorrectly, we can quickly become guilty of pastoral cross-cultural malpractice.

One way we see culture played out and fought over among Christians is in the area of worship. I am a conservative pastor who believes the Bible. I don't think culture changes the Bible's essential meaning, but it helps me understand what Scripture writers meant and helps me apply their teaching. In other words, I can't escape the idea that the psalmist was physically engaged in worship, and that worship for King David was not simply cerebral but also emotional. David even acknowledged that he might be despised for such an open display of exuberant worship, but he wasn't worried about it (see 2 Sam. 6:16–23).

I find it odd that Reformed pastors so often condemn the physical and emotional. They have no biblical basis for it. They think the way to protect the church from displays of emotion and physicality is to make rules against it. They take pastoral issues and make them theological ones by writing into Scripture that which is not there.

Their entire argument is actually a prejudice born out of their ethnic and national backgrounds. Unfortunately, they attempt to justify it with pseudo-theological and biblical rationalizations. Their last refuge is tradition or heritage, which just screams "culture." What bothers me about these culturally based positions is that they cut off fellowship, lead to a divisive spirit, and support others in their ignorance.

I don't condemn anyone for having preferences in worship. Some things might be found in Scripture, and thus biblical, but that doesn't necessarily mean I am automatically comfortable with them in my cultural context because I am not used to them. Some things tend to bother me because I am a man of routine and don't like surprises, even if they are positive and benign. For example, one day I preached at a Sudanese refugee camp in Uganda. We were met on the road a quarter-mile away from the church with flags, signs, cheering, and singing. And that was just the beginning. I enjoyed preaching to them; they were so responsive and emotional as they took in the Word of God. When I finished my sermon, there was an uproar; everyone broke into singing, rushed the podium, grabbed me, put me on their shoulders, and carried me around the outside of the building. Suffice it to say, that has never happened to me in America!

In fact, the opposite pattern is usually true for Americans. Sometimes White Americans haven't said one word to me after I thought I had preached my heart out, barely looking at me as they left the building. Later I found out that many were moved by the preaching, but not so much that it showed on the outside. I snicker when I hear preachers say, "We are clapping in our hearts." I have even heard pastors demand that their people stop clapping in a service. This would sound strange to the Jews, and it sounds strange to many ethnic people. Emotions are often culturally patterned and differ between various ethnic groups.

I have been in White services when someone sang a tremendously moving song. I could tell the whole congregation was emotionally affected. At the end of the song, the people could not help but burst into applause. The pastor quickly yelled, "Stop! We don't do that here." Apparently this is what someone captured by a cognitive culture felt he must do to keep worship dignified.

I don't think anything the Sudanese did the day I was there was unbiblical. To a White American anything that draws attention to an individual seems wicked, perhaps because White Americans think it better to be modest than to accept praise. White Americans value self-deprecation, whereas African Americans value the celebration of accomplishments, even small ones. Church leaders need to be culturally competent as they seek to pastor people, and especially if they are going to cross any cultural or ethnic lines to do it.

CULTURAL COMPETENCY

*I am obligated both to Greeks and non-Greeks, both to
the wise and the foolish. That is why I am so eager
to preach the gospel also to you who are in Rome.*
Romans 1:14–15

Cultural competency is something foreign missionaries are
supposed to be good at, and thankfully many do learn how to be
culturally competent or at least culturally adequate. Unfortunately
even some missionaries have failed to appreciate the cultural
nuances of the ethnic group to whom they wish to take the Gospel
of Christ. In a nation that has become one of the most ethnically
diverse in the history of the world, in the sense that our nation has
representatives from almost every other nation in it, it is important
for American pastors to think culturally in regard to both ethnicity
and economics if they want to reach people in different segments of
the population.

The standard for overseas missionaries used to be that they would
spend the first year or two in language and cultural learning. Many

today might feel like that was a waste of time. But to live among a new people group and not study their culture is an insult. Learning a language from Rosetta Stone is not a replacement for cultural learning.

In the American church we spend more time analyzing generational cultures than we do ethnic cultures. We want to know what age group you are in so we can analyze your generation and better understand how you think and what your pattern of behavior is. If we don't classify someone according to age group, we want to know where to place them on the Myers-Briggs test so we know whether they are an introvert or an extrovert. All this is valuable to some degree, but it is only part of what makes people tick.

Some might think: "This generation is not as subject to prejudice as previous generations; they are all multicultural." But this is not the case and again reveals an ignorance of the power of ethnicity and class.

Most in the majority and dominant White culture have little idea of what it is like to live as a minority in our nation. We neither understand the pain of being insulted, overlooked, and dismissed because of our physical appearance, nor do we appreciate the pain of history. We miss the relevance of historic racism and how it relates to immediate events of injustice against members of a minority group. Some in the majority culture are racist on purpose, while many are blithely ignorant of their privilege (*all* dominant cultures in a society have privilege, no matter their personal hardships) and feel insulted when it is pointed out.

Becoming cross-cultural or culturally competent can be a painful journey of humility. It is a journey of listening to voices that sound hurt or angry, of repenting, and of accepting both forgiveness and responsibility. But being cross-culturally competent is also wonderful, enriching, expanding, and full of love. It is worth the trouble!

A biblical strategy for cross-cultural missions can be found in 1

Corinthians 9:19–23 from the Apostle Paul, the great cross-cultural missionary:

For though I am free from all, I have made myself a servant to all, that I might win more of them. To the Jews I became as a Jew, in order to win Jews. To those under the law I became as one under the law (though not being myself under the law) that I might win those under the law. To those outside the law I became as one outside the law (not being outside the law of God but under the law of Christ) that I might win those outside the law. To the weak I became weak, that I might win the weak. I have become all things to all people, that by all means I might save some. I do it all for the sake of the gospel, that I may share with them in its blessings.

Loving your neighbor as yourself can be more complicated in a multiethnic and multicultural environment. Sometimes what I think is an expression of love is actually misunderstood by someone from another language or cultural group. Can I hug you, or does my touch repel and frighten you? Can I look you in the eye, or is that intimidating? Does my racial and ethnic group convey danger and threat to you simply by my presence and will it take time for you to trust me, or do you give trust readily because of the way I look? Do my emotional reactions alarm you, or do yours alarm me because I misinterpret them?

Love presses on. It seeks to know and be known because it wants a relationship. Love does not give up, even sometimes when it is rejected, insulted, or misunderstood. Love *becomes* in the same way Jesus became flesh and dwelt among us. Jesus came to the world, and the world knew him not. He came to his own, and his own received him not. Yet he kept coming, and he keeps coming: *"Yet to all who did receive him, to those who believed in his name, he gave the right to become children of God"* (John 1:12).

SUGGESTIONS

1. Know who you are and where you come from and be secure in that identity. Paul knew who he was in Christ (notice what he says about his relationship to the Law), and that enabled him to make himself a slave to others. Insecurity in your own identity will make you resistant to appreciating, understanding, or adapting to someone else's culture.

2. Have the goal to win others from a particular culture. The goal is not simply to understand or empathize but to *win* others, even those from resistant cultures, to the Savior. Failure to remember this goal of seeking to win people to Christ in cross-cultural ministry will cause you to wander and become confused about your purpose.

3. Crossing cultures is a process of becoming. It is an intentional, purposeful, and dedicated pursuit of listening to, learning from, engaging with, and feeling the pain, aspirations, hopes, and dreams of another culture.

4. Crossing cultures for the sake of Christ and to win

others to Christ is an intentional process of becoming a "slave" to that people group. It is not becoming a casual and distant observer, nor a tourist, and not even a cultural anthropologist, but a slave.

5. As worthy as they might be, it is not for the sake of the people that you engage but for the sake of the Gospel. This is important to remember, because along this cultural journey you might suffer culture shock, cultural fatigue, or even cultural alienation. How can you continue to serve and love people when you find there is much about them you don't like? It might be that you need to take a closer look at your own sins and those of your people group. More importantly, take a fresh look at Jesus Christ and let his love be your compelling force!

6. Crossing cultures for Jesus' sake is a way of loving people. Some have to be cross-cultural as a form of survival since they live as minorities in a dominant culture. As Christians we become more than immigrants, more than sojourners, and even more than a minority in any culture in which we might live. We are to be neighbors, and that means we must love the people around us for Jesus' sake.

PART EIGHT
SELF AWARENESS
MINISTERING FOR THE LONG HAUL

Watch your life and doctrine closely. Persevere in them, because if you do, you will save both yourself and your hearers.
1 Timothy 4:16

I want to share some thoughts on the soul, body, and emotions of the pastor. I thought too little about these issues in my youth and early years in the ministry. I was amazingly arrogant about my ability to do ministry. I was in self-denial about many of my sins and addictions. I was neglectful of my wife and young family. I gave little thought to longevity or being sustained for the long haul. In fact, I idealistically thought it would be better to "burn out for the Lord." I have since apologized to my wife, who I told I would probably burn out and die young serving the Lord. Yet here I still am. I hope she is not too disappointed!

I confess that far too much of my life as a student, husband, father, pastor, and Christian has been about "getting over and getting by." I often trusted in my giftedness to replace my lack of diligence, and because the Lord blessed me with talent and charisma I was able to hide it from many. May the Lord forgive me for not making more of myself, my time, and my opportunities. I am sorry to those who were hurt by my neglect.

What follows are lessons learned in self-care. More and more books are being written about these things, sometimes by men who have crashed and burned before learning hard lessons. There were few such books when I began my work as a pastor. I am happy there are more now.

Please take seriously these calls for your pastoral health. Please assume you are weak. Please don't assume you are above it all or have special powers to escape temptation or struggle. As Paul said, *"So, if you think you are standing firm, be careful that you don't fall!"* (1 Cor. 10:12). Solomon before him said, *"Do not be wise in your own eyes; fear the Lord and shun evil. This will bring health to your body and nourishment to your bones"* (Prov. 3:7–8).

A few years before I stepped down from my role as Senior Pastor of New City Fellowship, I was given the opportunity to be part of a cohort provided by Covenant Theological Seminary and funded by a grant from the Lilly Foundation. May God bless both of those institutions for the blessing that cohort experience provided for me and Joan! Our cohort was made up of pastors and their wives who had been in ministry for at least eighteen years, so we were an older, more experienced group. Age didn't mean any of us were the wiser, but at least we had more war stories to illustrate what we were learning.

Dr. Robert Burns at the seminary gave us great leadership as we examined our ministries through the reading of various books, special speakers, and group discussions. I recommend his book, *Resilient Ministry: What Pastors Told Us About Surviving and Thriving*,[1] which says that one of the most important ingredients to a pastor's life is his personal relationship with Christ. The lesson I learned as a teenager under my pastor about the need to have daily devotions or a "quiet time" has been my life support to sustain me in a lifetime of ministry.

During my years of ministry, I have faced various challenges to my personal endurance. I like to eat, and therefore have struggled with my weight. Thankfully, as a US Army Reserve Chaplain, I had to face a weigh-in twice a year as well as pass a physical fitness test (APFT). This accountability forced me to run and exercise and probably kept me alive. Obesity is a problem in our country, especially among the poor, and I was not always interested in eating healthy as I grew up. For a pastor, staying physically healthy is beneficial.

When I was young, I remember a few pastors who were very fat. It seemed as though everyone tried to ignore it and not say anything insulting. Today the culture is different, and we have lots of marathon-running pastors, iron men, CrossFit addicts, and jocks. Some of it, in fact, is past the point of being healthy and borders on its own addiction. I can fall in this camp. 1 Timothy 4:8 says, *"For physical training is of some value, but godliness has value for all things, holding promise for both the present life and the life to come."*

Pastors should make sure they get regular check-ups and see their doctors as needed. It would be great for any of us and our reputations if we were to die in the pulpit while preaching about heaven; it has happened. However, I suspect it would be appreciated by your wife, kids, and congregation if that happened after a lifetime of ministry and not in your middle years or sooner. If you are prone to depression, please see a counselor or doctor. If they give you a prescription, take it. You are not a failure if you struggle with feelings of despair or discouragement.

There is probably nothing better for your physical heart than to have a happy home life (Prov. 14:30, 15:30, 17:22). If you are in love with your wife, and she loves you, if you enjoy your children, and they delight for you to be home and involved in their lives, this is a joy indeed. If you are not married, consider how you might work toward good companionship.

The pastor's emotional stability in the midst of stress is very important. A pastor who cannot control his temper or hear bad news without an emotional collapse will cause his congregation to question whether he can handle difficulties in the power of the Spirit (see Ps. 112:7, Prov. 24:10).

Because pastors often think of themselves as apologists for the faith and protectors of doctrine, as well as moral guardians, they can be prone to contentiousness. If they like to argue, they may cause more problems than they solve. Paul gives guidance to Timothy that elders are not to be contentious (2 Tim. 2:24). This sounds like it was written especially for Presbyterians. If you are someone who is always fighting (over doctrine, church decisions, the worship service, the budget, or personnel issues), this might mean that you shouldn't be an elder.

A pastor has to keep his head in tough situations. He has to learn to answer kindly, lovingly, and with a sense of faith and optimism. There will be times when the appropriate response will be to lament and weep alongside those who are weeping. However, often the congregation will look to the pastor for faith and hope when hard circumstances fall (Prov. 24:10). Diagnosis for terminal disease will come, automobile accidents will happen, young people will go off to fight and die in wars, violence and crime will affect our families, some of our people will be murdered in the streets, mental illness will strike, and children will leave the faith. Where is the hope, where is a good word, where is there light at the end of the tunnel?

To this end, pastors need to have some emotional distance from situations that their members (and dear friends) will face. Some pastors cannot create that distance; they are prone to codependence and do not see a distinction between themselves and the people directly affected. This causes these pastors to bear a load they cannot carry. Sometimes only God can protect you when trouble strikes close to home. Some troubles can threaten the social and financial foundations of the church. If you do not maintain a prayer life, you are more likely to be eaten up by stress and perhaps even fold under the burden or burn out.

I hope the Lord has given you a sense of humor and that you

know how to have fun. I hope you have a sense of adventure, learning, or a positive spirit. I hope you know how to sing and that you sing a lot. I hope you know how to cry in public. I hope you know how to dance. Though wine can make the heart glad, I hope you avoid the trap of needing it to relax. Nehemiah 8:10 was an instruction for the people to enjoy some food and drink and not to keep grieving, but the bottom line was, *"The joy of the Lord is my strength."* May that be true for you as well!

I recommend that everyone in ministry read Paul Tripp's book *Dangerous Calling.*[2] I also recommend they read books by Peter Scazzero on emotionally healthy spirituality, churches, and leadership.[3] These authors speak powerfully about many of the struggles we have as ministers.

True Gospel ministry is a spiritual enterprise. Jesus has saved us; this is what it means to be a Christian, a believer, someone who is now born-again. Our sins have been forgiven, and we are indwelt by the Holy Spirit. The Spirit opened our eyes through regeneration and so we have been brought from spiritual death to life. We believed and have been declared righteous by faith. Through that act of justification we have been adopted and are now heirs of God and joint heirs with Christ. In Christ we are assured there is no condemnation for us due to our sins. We have been reconciled to God and reconciled to all of his children through the cross. Hallelujah!

So what is the problem? If we are now holy before God due to the imputation of the righteousness of Jesus Christ to our account (1 Cor. 5:21), and if God no longer counts our sins against us, then why should we feel guilty about any sinfulness on our part? The Bible says in 1 John 3:9, *"No one who is born of God will continue to sin, because God's seed remains in him; he cannot go on sinning because he has been born of God."* Does that mean we won't struggle with sin, or is there a difference between remaining in sin and struggling against it? If we struggle against it, do we refuse to claim it as a definition of ourselves in light of our sainthood, or do we engage the struggle and seek to use the resources of God to fight sin within ourselves?

A couple in my church began to study the idea of sanctification and the book of Romans. They complained about my seeming fixation on our sinfulness in my preaching. As I thought about it, I would have to say they had a point in observing a fixation about our struggle with sin. Every time we corporately confessed our sins, we were admitting as a whole church that we were still sinning, thus it would be fair to say we thought of ourselves as sinners.

This couple was bothered by that emphasis. They wondered why the verses in Jeremiah 17:9–10 were so often quoted, where it says, *"The heart is deceitful above all things and beyond cure. Who can understand it. I the Lord search the heart...."* They personally didn't like hearing this; it seemed to neglect the positive definition of ourselves in Christ as righteous. They didn't think Paul's statement that he was *"the chief of sinners"* had any relevance for the way we should look at ourselves or his comment in Romans 7:18, *"For I know that good itself does not dwell in me, that is, in my sinful nature."*

I was frustrated by their criticism. As a congregation we seemed to revel in our adoption as sons and daughters of God. We joyfully preached the forgiveness we have in Christ and the need to rid ourselves of any bondage to legalism. We summed up our philosophy of worship in one word: JOY!

However, the reality of our present sinfulness, especially the reality of my particular sinfulness, was inescapable to me. How could anyone honestly deny being tempted from time to time, sometimes failing, and always subject to the reality of the old nature? This couple seemed to deny any power of the old nature, though I am sure they continued to sin, even if they downgraded their sins. I am not saying they were bad people; they were normal people, who could still sometimes do bad.

If you interpret Romans 7 as a description of a non-Christian becoming a Christian, and not the description of the old nature or the flesh within the believer, I can see how one might reach that conclusion, although I think Paul speaks in present tense about the flesh, not the past. The reality of your life doesn't match the idea that you are simply and totally a saint and that you never, or rarely, sin. First John speaks both about a real moral and consistent change for those born of God and also about the reality of needing to confess and needing an advocate. Psalm 32 suggests the spiritual reality of needing confession and forgiveness.

We are blessed to be forgiven in salvation, but we must acknowledge our present sins or else why would Scripture bring up the need to confess? I also think non-Christians would think we were ridiculous for pretending that our transgressions didn't count as actual sins, but theirs did. If we no longer sin, we certainly shouldn't keep praying the Lord's Prayer!

It is spiritually dangerous to deny the power of indwelling sin. I take it by faith that God has broken its power to dominate me by and through the victory Jesus won at the cross. I am not the man I was before I came to Jesus, but that old self still has raging desires within me. Satan uses the desires of that old nature to lure and draw me into sin (James 1:13–15).

This practice of confessing our sins is a mark of our Reformed heritage, and it is deeply biblical. It is hard to communicate to someone else the power of indwelling sin and the deceitfulness of our own hearts if we deny that sin is much of a problem for us. Maybe the experience of other believers is different from mine; maybe they really are righteous a lot more of the time than I am. I am happy for them if that is so, but as we say around here: "I ain't feeling it." I wouldn't deny that others are more righteous than me except that I am convinced of our continued common sinfulness, both by my own experience and by what Scripture teaches. No matter how unpleasant it is to be in a church that keeps talking about the need to confess and examine ourselves as we come to the Lord's Table, it is actually liberating to know the blood of Jesus will never lose its power.

I have given some thought as to why I feel guilty from time to time. It is because... I sin from time to time. I can't deal with my sin by simply refusing to feel guilty. I see guilt (to some degree) as a gift. Guilt and sorrow are the things the Holy Spirit uses to bring me to conviction and repentance. As Paul Tripp says, we are in war, and the battle is over and about our hearts.[3]

I have no desire to wallow in my feelings of guilt; my only escape is to run to the cross and have my conscience sprinkled with the blood of Christ. My only hope is in remembering I have an advocate with the Father, Jesus Christ the righteous (1 John 2:1). As Romans 8 teaches us: *"Who will bring any charge against those whom God has chosen? ... Christ Jesus who died—more than that, who was raised to life—is at the right hand of God and is also interceding for us."* I am so blessed that nothing can separate me from the love of God which is in Christ Jesus our Lord. I encourage all pastors, and all believers, to read Romans 8 frequently.

I take Scripture seriously. I hear the warning that I not give way to a *"sinful, unbelieving heart that turns away from the living God"* (Heb. 3:12). If the Apostle Paul was convinced that he was purely a saint and without a sin struggle, then why did he talk about buffeting his body (1 Cor. 9:27)? I believe God will complete the work he has begun in me (Phil. 1:6), but I confess sometimes it seems I am on the edge of the cliff and hanging by a thread. At times I have been sin sick. I have no alternative but to keep crying out for God's mercy.

The pastor especially is on display as a warrior against his own sins. It is not that he should give us all the lurid details of his temptations, but for him to preach and act as if he has none is to set himself above the rest of the people and live a life of unreality and denial. Can you imagine interviewing a candidate for the job of pastor and asking him, "What are your struggles, your areas of besetting sin or weakness?" And what if he answered, "I am too hard on myself." Or, "I tend to always think the best of people, and I am too naive." Isn't that cute? I have heard applicants do this kind of thing. We should think, "Come on. Own up to the real you and stop trying to avoid the question!" I would say don't call such a person as a pastor until he learns to be honest.

We need to realize that we are dealing with pastors who are real people, real sinners, who still have areas of struggle. We are redeemed, and we need to live holy lives, but we are still very much human. We expect our pastors to be godly men, to seek after holiness. Yet without honesty there can be no true seeking after holiness, only pretense. Without humility, brokenness, and honesty there can be no repentance. Our churches are full of the disease of pretense. The people feel no safety in and from the church in dealing with their real sins except maybe in a generalized corporate confession.

So if the pastor is terrified of owning up to his sins, then the people will be as well. If the pastor can't relish the joy of his own forgiveness and testify continually to the mercy of God, why would the people trust that this God—and this church— would still receive them once the truth is found out about them? We must acknowledge the challenge between the struggle against sin and the confidence we have in God preserving us in our struggle. We must faithfully preach the Gospel of grace to our people—and to ourselves.

---

1. Robert Burns, Tasha Chapman, and Donald C. Guthrie, *Resilient Ministry: What Pastors Told Us About Surviving and Thriving* (Downers Grove, IL: InterVarsity Press, 2013).

2. Paul Tripp, *Dangerous Calling: Confronting the Unique Challenges of Pastoral Ministry*(Wheaton, IL: Crossway, 2012).

3. See Peter Scazzero with Warren Bird, *The Emotionally Healthy Church, Updated and Expanded Edition: A Strategy for Discipleship That Actually Changes Lives* (Grand Rapids, MI: Zondervan, 2010); Peter Scazzero, *The Emotionally Healthy Leader: How Transforming Your Inner Life Will Deeply Transform Your Church, Team, and the World* (Grand Rapids, MI: Zondervan, 2015); Peter and Geri Scazzero, *Emotionally Healthy Relationships Workbook: Discipleship that Deeply Changes Your Relationship with Others* (Grand Rapids, IL: Zondervan, 2017); Peter Scazzero, *Emotionally Healthy Spirituality: It's Impossible to Be Spiritually Mature, While Remaining Emotionally Immature*, upd. ed. (Grand Rapids, MI: Zondervan, 2017).

MANAGING DAILY RESPONSIBILITIES

Who of you by worrying can add a single hour to his life? Since you
cannot do this very little thing, why do you worry about the rest?
Luke 12:25–26

Time is another issue of self-care for pastors. Dealing with stress
through healthy habits of personal organization, through pre-plan-
ning, and by living in the power of faith and the Holy Spirit are
important tools to help a pastor endure in the ministry. The failure
to deal with stress won't make it go away. It may mean an ugly
confrontation at home with the family or possible conflict with
elders or members with whom you fail to keep appointments. It
might mean financial embarrassment or even a physical collapse.

When it comes to the area of time management in the day-to-day
life of ministry, there is much for all of us to learn so we can get
through our days without continuously frustrating ourselves or
others. One of the realities of pastoring is the our necessary availability (and flexibility) for emergencies. One cannot be a good
pastor for long and insist that you have a scheduled committee

meeting or have to work on your sermon and can't go to the hospital, jail, morgue, or scene of the accident.

Such flexibility means sometimes you must cancel appointments and meetings or postpone them. Sometimes it means you will fail to show up according to schedule. Sometimes you will be called back from a day off or family vacation. We live in the age of the cell phone, so there is hardly ever a reason people can't be informed as to what has kept you or will prevent you from coming. Try to protect your family time, but sooner or later you will have to leave the family and the house for an unexpected or unplanned situation. One suggestion I have is for you not to answer your phone during your evening meal if you are gathered as a family. You can check the message after dinner and call if necessary.

Inevitably, you must learn to limit yourself, especially if the scope of your responsibilities increases as the congregation grows. Will you take every sales call at the church office? Will you entertain every new book study, Bible study series, video training series, and Sunday School curriculum that vendors want the pastor to review and approve?

You simply cannot be available to everyone. Many sales and marketing people will not tell your secretary why they are calling. They want to get to you because they think you are the decision-maker for purchases, which is something you should learn to delegate. You will have to learn to dispense with sales people politely, lovingly, quickly, and firmly.

How about folks who aren't church members? For whom will you provide counseling? Which couples planning to get married will you work with and prepare? What committees will you join or not join? How will you handle the poor who come asking for help? Do you have a plan to minister to them (and not send them away) without making the pastor the "Sugar Daddy"? For more details, read my book about how to organize and train your congregation in mercy ministry—*Merciful: The Opportunity and Challenge of Discipling the Poor Out of Poverty*.[1]

You would be be wise to consider sitting down with your administrative assistant if you have one. Lay out a strategy so your time is protected, but yet you are available when true needs arrive. It is helpful to have stated office hours so people will know when you are available for calls and when you are not. You will not have enough study time, visitation time, and family or "you" time to get fed, exercised, and rested (or just to have fun) unless you schedule it. Whatever you do, you will have to live with some frustration, because invariably the systems will break down, someone won't follow policy, and you will violate your own rules. I guarantee it.

---

1. Randy Nabors, *Merciful: The Opportunity and Challenge of Discipling the Poor Out of Poverty*(North Charleston, SC: CreateSpace, 2015).

TIME AWAY

How often should a pastor be gone from his flock? How many outside engagements should a pastor take per year? How many Sundays should he miss for vacation, denominational responsibilities, or preaching invitations? The answer takes into account what your employer (your elders or board) allows, how many invitations you receive, and what you request (or need) for rest.

How many absences you should take from the pulpit is a slightly different question. There are times when the pastor is not out of town, but he opens the pulpit to a guest preacher, missionary, or associate pastor. Taken together with the pastor's absence from the church this can amount to a considerable amount of time away from his preaching presence and ministry. I know some pastors who are amazingly gifted and often were requested to speak but seldom leave their pulpits for out-of-town engagements. I know some who refused to share their pulpits, even with associate pastors who desperately needed preaching time. They wouldn't relinquish it for missionaries or special speakers. At the same time I have known some who always seemed to be gone, accepting any and all invitations to go somewhere else or be anywhere else than where their congregations expected them to be, which was at their own church preaching on Sundays.

The pastor who is always gone will most likely soon be gone—permanently. Congregations expect to be pastored by the pastor they have hired, and they expect that the person they pay to preach will actually do so on most Sundays. There are reasons some pastors are out of town or give their pulpit to others—some good and some not so good. The difficulty in discussing good and bad reasons is that sometimes these reasons are not obvious. A pastor may be having internal struggles, even deeply psychological ones, of which he is not consciously aware and hasn't come to grips with yet. So even if his absence looks legitimate, it may stem from a negative impulse.

If a pastor feels constantly criticized for his preaching, he may prefer to preach to people who don't complain or where he can preach one of his best sermons again and be fairly certain it will be well received. While his own people may seem bored to hear him week after week, other places may see him as a novelty and think he is exciting. Of course if he actually became their pastor, they might eventually be bored with him as well, so instead of resigning his charge he continues to use his main employment as a financial base but keeps traveling to get positive feedback from strangers. I personally loved preaching to my own congregation and seldom felt disappointed in their response or appreciation for my preaching. They seemed dismayed when I was gone and complained heartily if the person preaching in my absence was not very good.

Sometimes instead of the congregation being bored, the pastor may be bored and seek outside engagements because he loves novelty and varied experiences. This leads to the question of how much he really loves his flock, and does he seek to shepherd them effectively? If he only sees himself as a preacher and not a shepherd, then he won't care as much about shaping the congregation or discipling them toward the image of Christ.

I had an elder who loved me and liked my preaching. Sometimes he would come to session meetings with a list of dates that I had been absent from the pulpit. He was keeping score and would remind me of how much time I had missed. This always seemed to happen right before I was going to ask to be gone another Sunday! As annoying as this was to me, it was actually helpful. I hated saying no to anyone who asked me to come and preach because it boosted my ego and made me feel somewhat necessary for the advancement of the Kingdom of God. Being reminded that I had a responsibility to my home church gave me stability and kept me grounded in reality.

In my case, the session agreed that I would have a certain amount of time for vacation and another amount of time for my Army Reserve duty. If I exceeded that time, I would take an unpaid leave of absence. Unfortunately, a few times the Army took more time than planned when they sent me to war, but they then paid me and the church didn't have to do so. Special requests for my teaching or preaching from outside the congregation had to be filtered through a session committee that would permit, or not permit, another absence.

I was asked to do seminars in prisons, be a camp speaker, be a mission's conference speaker, take foreign mission trips, and more. Perversely, at the same time I often felt like nobody noticed me or invited me to the popular speaking opportunities. Most of this was an insatiable need within me to feel important. That was my fleshly desire, part of my sinful fallenness, a lack of faith in Christ's love for me, a failure to see and appreciate my true identity and worth in Christ, and the old-fashioned sin of pride. If I wasn't careful, I could use up all my vacation time going somewhere else to preach and then be exhausted. This ticked off my wife, but I was too embarrassed to complain to the elders that I needed more time off.

It is wise to make an agreement with your elders about how often you will be gone and also to have that agreement "policed." If a session doesn't hold preachers accountable, the spiritual nature of the pastor's calling can make all choices (i.e., to go somewhere else and preach) "God's will," even when it isn't. I am an advocate for rest, vacations, and sabbaticals. I believe pastors should participate in missions and extended study times. My problem was that I wanted to do it all, and my congregation's problem was they simply wanted a reliable pastor. Imagine that.

MONEY

I rejoiced greatly in the Lord that at last you have renewed your concern for me. Indeed, you have been concerned, but you had no opportunity to show it. I am not saying this because I am in need, for I have learned to be content whatever the circumstances. I know what it is to be in need, and I know what it is to have plenty. I have learned the secret of being content in any and every situation, whether well fed or hungry, whether living in plenty or in want. I can do everything through him who gives me strength.
Philippians 4:10–13

What an amazing lesson to learn, to be content in any and every situation. One of the greatest enemies of contentment is envy. We look around and see others with more than us, being more applauded, or given more opportunities. Our envy turns to bitterness, against others and against God while our whole sense of self is threatened. We stop believing that God loves or cares about us. Our sense of competition is stimulated. Instead of learning from others' successes, we feel jealous. Envy is an insidious enemy to the preacher's spiritual health. Again, *"A heart at peace gives life to the body, but envy rots the bones"* (Prov. 14:30).

With whom do you get angry when you don't have enough money? Do you get mad at God, the elders, the congregation, your wife, yourself? Money, the need and desire for it, does strange things to people. When we are lacking in resources we can become afraid and worry. That anxiety can easily spill into self-pity or anger. It is one thing to be a layperson who is frustrated with his or her boss due to a lack of adequate remuneration, but what do you do when the people of God are those who are supposed to pay your salary? Jesus taught us:

> *Then Jesus said to his disciples: "Therefore I tell you, do not worry about your life, what you will eat; or about your body, what you will wear. Life is more than food, and the body more than clothes. Consider the ravens: They do not sow or reap, they have no storeroom or barn; yet God feeds them. And how much more valuable you are than birds!"* Luke 12: 22–24

Pastors and ministry leaders often take unhelpful approaches to this problem. If you are blessed to have a comfortable income, then maybe you will have no appreciation for this issue. Take heed that someday your real character traits might be revealed if and when you fall into financial stress.

SUGGESTIONS

1. Don't make an idol out of your home life. Your wife and family should see you leading them to something greater than time with you and all of your attention. The call of God, missions, ministry, a commitment to a local church, justice, the poor, and love for others should be the value system on which our families are built. If you don't want self-centered children, you need to model living for more than self. Our demand for a good quality of life is often nothing but self-love.

2. If you are married, love your wife. If you want your children to respect you, then honor your wife. If you want respect from your wife, then learn to listen to her and take her opinions seriously. If you want your children to be polite, then teach them to respect and honor their mother. Insist on obedience and respect in the home from your children and do not allow signs and acts of rebellion in their early years to go unchecked. This discipline will pay off when they are teens.

3. Control your anger at home. Many pastors are driven

people, often frustrated, and sometimes too demanding of their wives and children. Yelling, being controlling, calling them names, and being overly strict does not equal "disciplining your children." Rather, love and patience with affection work wonders.

4. Nothing can replace time spent with your wife and kids. It is a rare pastor who can get through life without feeling guilty for the times missed with his immediate family. There is no way out of it; you and your family will sacrifice to be in the ministry, and you should. However, that means the times you set apart to be with them should be sacred to you. Set apart the time and fight hard to protect it. I failed often at this, as do many pastors (and others). But fight to protect that time.

5. Learn how to rest. Set a day off and take it. Plan vacations and take them. Ask for a sabbatical and use it well. Try not to have every vacation be a working vacation, though I realize sometimes that is the only way to get your family out of town and to some place fun. I learned these lessons far too late in raising a family. I am grateful for every memory of fun time off we had.

6. Pray for and practice a healthy sex life. If you are married, you must not neglect each other, nor be obsessive and selfish. Talk to your wife about your mutual needs and don't fall into habits of neglect or emotional distance.

7. May God deliver you from pornography! If it is any kind of problem, get counseling and help immediately. Protect yourself from temptation and don't think you are above it. Watch out for pastoral counseling sessions with women who are emotionally needy; make sure someone else is around or in the building. When you travel for ministry, take someone with you

(of the same sex or your wife) who will hold you to godly behavior. Think of yourself as vulnerable and a target for the devil. Don't listen to his lies that you deserve to be admired and can handle sexually dangerous situations.

8. Stop obsessing over money and worrying about how you are going to make it financially. It is easy to be angry about how little you are being paid, or how your children are missing out, or the car you have to drive, or the vacations you can't take. Pray about your money, be diligent to account for it and use it well, get advice on how to manage and budget it, but learn to be content in whatever situation you are in. Make sure you tithe faithfully and be generous. Stop complaining (especially in front of your wife) and be grateful. It is unhealthy to have a cheap and greedy heart. As Proverbs 14:30 says, *"Envy rots the bones."*

9. The way you think about money, spend money, give money, go into debt, or complain about money is not simply a symptom of your wealth but of your spiritual health.

10. Resources come from God, not people, and as soon as you forget that you are in trouble. Anger, self-pity, or blame-shifting is not a sign or testimony of faith.

11. "Poor mouthing" to the congregation about your financial problems from the pulpit is manipulation and not a sign of integrity. A preacher has the power to use the pulpit to get members to give him private gifts, over and above his agreed compensation, and this is a shameful practice.

12. It is necessary and right to clearly communicate to those who decide on your income about your financial situation and your need for more compensation if necessary. How you communicate your needs will tell

them much about the condition of your heart and will either increase their loyalty to you or drive them away.

13. You need to decide whether you are a "hireling" or an "owner" of the ministry to which God has called you. If you are simply an employee, you will think like one, grieve when not rewarded adequately, complain, blame the church, and eventually forfeit your right to lead them.

14. You are expected to call the people to discipleship in their giving, but you must practice what you preach and lead by example. If you call for sacrifice and faithfulness in giving or tithing, then you'd better be doing it too.

15. It is good and necessary to develop relationships with the wealthy members of your church, as with everyone. Relationships with wealthy people means you can encourage them to be rich in good deeds. If they seek to help you personally that is a blessing as long as it is legal and without compromise of the ministry of the Word. However, if you direct their primary giving to yourself and not the ministry, then you are being unethical. Definitely don't hide income from the government.

16. If you are married with a family, then your family has to share in your faith and not drive you to fear or anger because you can't meet their demands. Your qualification for leadership is revealed in the way you lead your family. If you do not have the faith or the ability to live under the terms of the call you received, either refuse to accept it or seek to renegotiate it. If your employer is too cheap or hard-hearted to adequately support you, you may need to find some other place to labor.

17. Don't translate as a lack of God's or your congregation's

care for you your frustration with finances due to your consumer wants (including paying for Christian education), consumer debt, or unforeseen medical or other expenses. Stop comparing yourself with the wealthiest members of the church and start comparing yourself with the poorest. If God takes care of sparrows, he will take care of you. Trust him!

18. No two congregations are the same, so you should be very careful about salary comparisons. Envy and coveting are not good motives to jack up your salary. If you think the primary financial mission of the congregation is to keep you in a comfortable lifestyle, you have missed what the church is supposed to be about. Your quality of life goals—the size of your house, year/make/model of your car, private school for your kids, etc.—are not the responsibility of your church. They are perks, blessings, things to save and strive for, but not leverage for you to demand more income from your congregation.

19. You are worthy of your hire, and it is right that the congregation should strive to adequately take care of you and your family. However, you must measure the pressure you put on them to support you with the understanding that believers should not give to God out of necessity or compulsion but with cheerfulness. Part of their cheerfulness will come from seeing how gracious and loving you are, especially when you are stressed about money.

20. Figure out how to worship as a family and instruct your children in the faith. Use the catechism, Scripture memory, Psalms, hymns, spiritual songs, Christian stories, biographies, devotionals, and the Bible itself. Engage your children in ministry events, mission trips, and service. Pray with and for them, at the table, when

you put them to sleep, when they are struggling with issues with friends, at school, etc.

21. Compliment, encourage, and speak positively to your children. Try to say yes more often than you say no. Make sure your wife and you are a team and can't be divided and conquered by your children. Reward, gently push, ask questions, listen to their questions, and do not rush to judge them for doubts or concerns. Brag about them, and let them know of your pride in them. Say "I love you" a lot. Let your boundaries be clear and the door always open to your heart.

22. Make sure your weeks of vacation, study leave, and future sabbatical are actually in your stated call or contract. Remember that unless your elders or members are in an academic setting, the concept of a sabbatical may be foreign to them. You will need to educate your leadership as to why a sabbatical is both good for you and for the church.

23. If you apply for a sabbatical, it is wise to come to your leadership with a plan about how it will be funded, who will fill the pulpit, and who will be the point person for pastoral care while you are gone. You should be clear in your own mind what your goals are for the sabbatical. Is it rest, personal study, exposure to other and new ministries, training, education, or writing a book? Make sure you know what you want to get out of it because it will go by all too quickly. I have known several pastors who asked for a sabbatical *after* they felt burned out. I encourage you to plan ahead for a sabbatical *before* you feel burned out. Hopefully regular rest and refreshment can prevent you from feeling burned out at all. Some pastors have used their sabbaticals to decide to resign from the church and announced it when they returned. This might not be

fair to the church, especially if the pastor is pretty sure he wants out. It might be more fair in such a case to simply ask for the time as severance. Churches may allow their pastors to have a sabbatical to sort through personal, family, or theological issues with the full awareness that a staff change might be coming. Honest communication is important.

CONCLUSION

Pastoring well is difficult work. The emotional burden can be crushing, the moral standards daunting, the performance demands constant, and the battering experience of criticism devastating. When added to the challenges of being a good spouse or parent while living in the glass house of ministry, the demands and attendant guilt can be not only frustrating but demoralizing. Unfortunately, the more driven a pastor is, the faster the acceleration of the ministry train can be. Left unchecked, this train can cause a pastor to crash and burn, especially if he is already prone to depression.

I have tried to speak realistically about the challenges of ministry. So many pastors pursue a call to ministry but don't make it past Year 5. Very few make it for a lifetime. The odds go up if a pastor is in a denomination that requires training, provides accountability, and offers some measure of support. The odds also go up if a pastor is privileged to shepherd a church that has loving and loyal leadership that cares for both the pastor as a person and for the congregation.

Few people would neglect maintenance on their home, car, or tools if they valued them. Pastors need maintenance as well.

In my experience, pastors are too often either kept poor financially and made to feel insecure in their leadership by a critical congregation or paid too much and idolized by their followers without the accountability and reality checks that we all need to be kept honest.

All in all let me affirm that a call to the preaching and pastoral ministry is one of the greatest callings a person can receive. I believe that when I preach I am to speak *"as an oracle of God"* (1 Pet. 4:11). What an amazing privilege! I am not greater than other men, but I do believe that what I do as a pastor is not ordinary work. It is holy work, and people's souls depend upon it. Some may seek to make every task equal, trying to protect us from a sacred-secular dichotomy. And I agree that every task should be done for the glory of God, and thus all of life is holy in that sense. But not every task snatches souls from hell, preserves God's people for heaven, builds the church, and heals wounded hearts. In that sense, shepherding souls is a high calling that we should seek to do with all humility and diligence.

I hope I have not discouraged you, for the task of ministering the Gospel is indeed a special one. But the Gospel ministry, the pastoral call, and the gifts of pastor/teacher are given to real flesh and blood people. We are all insufficient in fulfilling that office and calling, no matter how much public success we have enjoyed. In my case, there were times my ego, confidence, and arrogance were unjustifiably above my capacity, until those moments when I came crashing back to earth and had to face reality. Humiliation was what I needed and what God provided. I found out that God does indeed give grace to the humble.

Others approach the ministry with fear and feelings of helplessness. But they actually have more capacity than they realize. Whatever the gap between your sense of ability and your capacity, I want to encourage you that Jesus is the one that makes the difference.

The healthiest thing for all of us is to learn how to identify our weaknesses and then find grace from God and our strength in and from him. There is a wonderful promise in 2 Corinthians 9:8 that should encourage all of us insufficient folk involved in ministry: *"And God is able to bless you abundantly, so that in all things at all times, having all that you need, you will abound in every good work."* Look at the scope of this promise: all things, at all times, all that you need! So there is neither time, nor place, nor any problem that God is not able to help us in the work to which he has called us.

May the Lord Jesus make us all more like himself! May his Holy Spirit take your weak and insufficient self and empower you through his grace to be holy and to live holy. May he give you endurance in the calling you have received to be a pastor. May he give you love for your people and effectiveness in serving them for Jesus. If you are married, may he give you a stable and believing family whose children grow up to confess and love the Lord, no matter how hard your charge has been. May he make you a great preacher of a full and wonderful Gospel. And may you believe the Gospel for yourself and thrive in its power to save, deliver, and continue to change you!

APPENDIX: THE APOSTLES' CREED

I believe in God, the Father almighty,
creator of heaven and earth.
I believe in Jesus Christ, God's only Son, our Lord,
who was conceived by the Holy Spirit,
born of the Virgin Mary,
suffered under Pontius Pilate,
was crucified, died, and was buried;
he descended to the dead.
On the third day he rose again;
he ascended into heaven,
he is seated at the right hand of the Father,
and he will come to judge the living and the dead.
I believe in the Holy Spirit,
the holy catholic Church,
the communion of saints,
the forgiveness of sins,
the resurrection of the body,
and the life everlasting. Amen.

APPENDIX: WEDDINGS

I'll make general comments about weddings before I give a typical outline of a wedding service. Please insist on premarital counseling and make sure your elders or leadership agree with the policy.

Be aware of scheduling issues for weddings versus church life. Will you perform a wedding on a holiday? What about your own family plans? What about Sundays, Christmas, New Year's Eve or Day, Easter, etc.? Weddings are usually more than one day's activity for a pastor if you count the rehearsal and rehearsal dinner. Prepare to be the wedding director if your church doesn't have one or the wedding party doesn't secure one. Otherwise you'll invite chaos, arguments, and a long evening prior to the wedding.

Coordinate with your church's leadership about the cost of weddings—the use of the building, musicians, custodians, the kitchen, flowers, etc. Try to have these costs posted, published, and agreed to by the wedding party. Any other policies the church has (about alcohol, dancing, etc.) should be known by the wedding party. Make sure you agree on who will supply the printed program if there is to be one. Hopefully you will have the support of the church to provide a wedding for little or no cost for those who have no money or family to support them.

Try to help the wedding party be reasonable about photographs. Will they do all the photos ahead of time, after the wedding, during, or all three? Feel free to lay down the rules about what you will allow in terms of photographers interacting during the service. Some couples have no idea how long the day will become, or how the reception will be delayed, or how exhausted they will be due to the requirements of photographers.

A Sample Wedding Service

Seating of family and parents (Musical elements)
Pastor and Groom and Best Man take their place
Processional of Maids and Groomsmen
Bridal march
Welcome and Declaration of the Day
Invocation
Giving of the Bride
Hymn or Song
Vows of Intent ("Do you" or "Will you")
Solo or Music
Rise to the platform or altar
Scripture Reading
Homily
Wedding Vows (There are good options for these.)
Prayers of dedication
Giving of the rings
Prayer
Pronouncement of marriage
Kiss
Benediction
Introduction of Couple

Recessional March

Unity Candles
Jumping of the broom
Flowers to the parents
Parents come up to pray blessing on the couple

Various designs of how bride's maids and groomsmen come in, where they stand, and how they exit. Ring bearer, flower girls, and plans for participation of little children. Who will direct their entry and control them?

If multiple pastors are involved, who will do what? Pay attention to the possibility that some might overstep their place and decide to give a mini-sermon. Pay attention to fathers who are also ministers and how they might feel about their role in the service.

Will announcements need to be given about how to recess, or where to go for the reception, or what the wedding couple asks of family for photographs, etc.?

Make sure the marriage license gets signed and mailed.

APPENDIX: FUNERALS

In this appendix I give at least one possible outline of an order of service for a funeral. Here are few comments about preparation for a funeral.

There are various ways a pastor gets involved with a funeral. The first of course is visiting or calling the family who has lost a loved one. This should always be pursued by a pastor when it is a member of the church or a family member of a church member. There is a period when a pastor is not sure if he or the church will be asked to do or host the funeral. Once the request has been made, there is a period when the grieving family may or may not need guidance on what to do. Some families take charge to call a funeral home, pick a date, choose a burial place, etc. The more prepared and organized the family is the easier things will be for the pastor—just agree on the time, place, and what will happen in the service.

Other families have no idea what to do. Pastors should have contact with local funeral homes and be willing to go with a survivor to help make funeral decisions (place of funeral, casket, wake, repast, plot, cost, and program). It is not the pastor's place to make these decisions but to provide whatever pastoral presence or wisdom during the shock and confusion in these days. Pastors can offer the church facility, ideas for the program, musicians and choir, a reception, etc. if they have access to those resources and the support of the church.

In the Black community there are usually different pastors who have connections with a family, and the host pastor may wish to invite these pastors up on the platform, distribute some part of the service to them, or ask them to "give a word."

Pay attention to timing for the grave site. Military cemeteries have a definite time schedule both to begin and end, which means the funeral motorcade must leave the church in time to make the appointment.

Outline of Service

Gathering of Family—prayer with family before processional

Processional—coordinate with Funeral Director as to pre-placed casket in the sanctuary or family follows in behind it. In the Black church one of the pastors usually precedes or leads the family in while reading relevant Scriptures to bring the family into the sanctuary. Musicians or choir provides the processional music.

View or Not to View—Some families wish this to be the last viewing (if it is an open casket). I recommend against this as it is too emotional, and it is difficult to get the service started as one doesn't want to be too directive as a family grieves over their loved one. Hopefully this last viewing can be done at the wake, or in the pre-service visitation time.

Welcome—usually the host pastor

Call to Worship and Invocation

Music—Can be a hymn or choir number

Scripture Reading—Can be Old Testament and New Testament or just one

Remembrances, Eulogy, or Resolutions—Some families wish an open microphone for anyone who wishes to say something (I strongly suggest that a pastor supervise this and limit the time for each person as this can drag on and even get subverted by people who wish to make a scene). Some families have appointed representatives to give remembrance or read a poem. In the Black church there are often formal resolutions given by the church or churches which have some historical or family connection. A eulogy is a presentation of "good words" about the life of the deceased often given by a family member, close friend, or a pastor.

Solo, Music, or Special Presentation

Scripture for Sermon—It is good to ask the family if there is a favorite passage of the deceased or the survivors. Whatever they say, make sure you preach the Gospel.

Sermon

Announcement for Graveside

Recessional—Music by choir or instrumentalists.

ABOUT THE AUTHOR

Randy Nabors is Pastor Emeritus of New City Fellowship in Chattanooga, Tennessee, where he planted and served for thirty-six years. During that time he also served as a US Army Reserve Chaplain with several deployments overseas in the Gulf wars and was given a two-year leave to serve as a missionary pastor in Nairobi, Kenya.

Randy serves as Coordinator of Urban and Mercy Ministries for Mission to North America of the Presbyterian Church in America. He also serves as the Coordinator of the New City Network, an affinity network of congregations and ministries that follow the model of New City Fellowship in Chattanooga—urban, cross-cultural, inclusive of the poor, joyful worship, and sound biblical teaching. He and his wife Joan travel to counsel, coach, encourage, train, and develop pastors and congregations in the works of mercy, justice, and cross-cultural ministry and worship.

Randy and Joan grew up in Newark, New Jersey, and are graduates of Covenant College. Randy earned his MDiv from Covenant Theological Seminary. They have four grown children and twelve grandchildren. Randy is the author of *Merciful: The Opportunity and Challenge of Discipling the Poor Out of Poverty.* To learn more about the New City Network, visit www.thenewcitynetwork.org.